Farm Girl
Country Cooking

Hearty Meals
for the Active Family

Books by Karen Jones Gowen

Farm Girl

Uncut Diamonds

House of Diamonds

Lighting Candles in the Snow

Farm Girl Country Cooking

Hearty Meals
for the Active Family

Karen Jones Gowen

WiDō Publishing • Salt Lake City

WiDō Publishing
Salt Lake City, Utah
widopublishing.com

Print ISBN: 978-1-937178-37-6
Library of Congress Control Number: 2013939285

Cover design by Don Gee
Photography by Erin Gowen
Book design by Marny K. Parkin

Printed in the United States of America

To Bruce,
who loves to eat and forever appreciates my culinary efforts,
and all of my creative endeavors

About This Cookbook

Although preparing regular family meals can be difficult, it is worth every effort. Dinner provides an opportunity to gather and refresh while spending time together around the table enjoying a meal.

Karen Jones Gowen has collected and tested the book's 100 recipes of main dishes, sides and desserts from years of experience cooking for a large family. Whether you're feeding a family on a budget or need ideas on menu planning, this cookbook is the perfect companion for the busy, working cook.

Hearty home-cooking using basic ingredients, plenty of fresh vegetables (and don't forget the bacon) you will return to these recipes again and again when planning dinners for your family or entertaining for company.

Contents

My mother as a young girl in Nebraska, from the book Farm Girl *(WiDō Publishing, 2007).*

A social gathering at the Marker family farm in Nebraska. My grandmother would serve cake, home-made ice cream, lemonade and coffee at these parties.

Introduction

I didn't begin domestic life knowing how to cook, or even liking it. What a messy, tedious, time-consuming, endless, thankless task is preparing daily meals for a growing, hungry family. If there had been a way to get out of it, I'd have surely done it.

Karen Jones and Bruce Gowen Wedding Day, August 13, 1970; Oakland, California.

Like if my husband enjoyed cooking. Or if we had the money to go out to eat every day. Or to hire a cook. Or if our in-laws lived with us. My mother-in-law was a wonderful cook. When she visited we had an arrangement—she'd cook and I'd clean up—because I'd rather clean the kitchen than cook the meal.

Not that cleaning was my talent either. But I'd gladly clean the kitchen back then if someone else did the cooking.

I started married life with a few items I enjoyed making: cookies, cake and home-made bread. My challenge was to figure out how to fill in the missing pieces and provide complete and balanced meals. Day after day after day.

My mother grew up on a farm, where cooking was a part of the daily routine. Meat, potatoes, vegetables, home-made bread. And that culture was ingrained into my family. You grow vegetables, you plan meals, you prepare food for the family. I took it all for granted when I was a kid. Then I got married and realized it was now my job. I had a lot to learn!

There I was with a husband who went to work, repaired our cars, did the yard work, fixed everything that broke, but didn't cook. Small children who

The Gowen Family, Christmas 1981.

Karen in the kitchen.

ingredients, processed ready-made food that always cost more. The more treatment a food item gets, the higher the consumer cost. Packaged salad mix costs more than a head of lettuce. Instant mashed potatoes costs more per serving than a ten pound bag. You get the idea. To stretch our limited finances I had to peel and grate and chop and squeeze and simmer and sauté and stir and do it all myself.

And so I became extremely choosy about what recipes I used. They had to fit certain criteria: inexpensive, take the least time possible, nutritious, tasty, filling.

My husband is over six feet tall, and we had many sons, all of whom were growing fast and needing calories on a regular basis. I grew up with three sisters, no brothers, and had no idea of the quantities of food a healthy male appetite could consume.

I learned that the hearty meals of my farm girl mother, my farmer grandparents and aunts were well-suited for the active group of sons and daughters that we were raising. Our children were our main crop, and the family recipes I developed over the years helped them to grow up healthy and strong, while maintaining my own sanity. I hope they will benefit your family as well.

The recipes are all connected, with suggestions on what to serve with what. I hope you'll feel comfortable changing them around, tweaking the ingredients, and making them suitable for you and your family's needs, just as I did through the years.

Happy meal time!

didn't cook. No live-in relatives to cook for us. No extra money to eat out or even to buy ready-made dinners in a box.

Clearly it was up to me.

Being on a very strict food budget didn't help. The "I hate to cook" recipes out there use canned

A Healthy, Balanced Way of Feeding the Family:
How to Use This Cookbook

This book is for the working cook. For the busy person who wants to prepare regular family meals but really doesn't have the time, energy or interest to pull it off. And buying ready-made ingredients to make super-quick meals is killing your food budget. What to do?

I feel your pain. I've been there. And through the years I collected and revised my own recipes and methods to create the family dinners that kept my food budget in control and my family satisfied. Each recipe in this cookbook has been tested on our own large family and passed certain criteria:

- Fast
- Filling
- Nutritious
- Delicious
- Inexpensive
- Easily doubled or tripled
- Simple directions that allow kids to help with the cooking

In addition, I use a lot of fresh vegetables, varied according to season, whole grains, a variety of seasonings and spices, alternative protein sources and less meat. This is what keeps the meals nutritious, inexpensive and still delicious and satisfying.

A big part of meal preparation is knowing what to fix with what. Have you ever prepared a main dish and forgot to fix anything to go with it? Or get busy with other things and run out of time? You go to considerable trouble to make a dish, isn't that enough? Apparently not, because when it's gone in three minutes, and everyone looks around expectantly for something else; well, that's not very fun for anyone, especially the cook.

These main dish recipes come with serving suggestions of side dishes, all recipes included. I've also included different suggestions on the side dishes for variety, so there's more than one meal combination idea. Start out with three to five complete meals for dinners and expand from there, until you have a repertoire of dinner menus you can pull together that meet you and your family's needs and schedules. Many of the menus are also suitable for company dinners.

The Rule of Three

The best way to use this cookbook is to select a main dish, add a salad, bread or carbohydrate, and then a dessert if you wish. Four items at every meal makes a nice meal, five makes a feast.

Most of our family meals had three items, following the Rule of Three, which I found to be the ideal number for physical and emotional satisfaction at dinner. Less than three items and it seemed more like a snack than a meal. Four or five items provide a sense of abundance—nice occasionally, but not what I wanted them to expect at every meal!

The three items don't need to be elaborately created from scratch; you might open a can of applesauce to add to a sandwich and a glass of milk. Three items, it's a meal. A hot dog by itself seems like a snack but top with chili, add orange slices to the side, and ice cream for dessert, you've got a meal.

The Rule of Three also helped me create guidelines for teaching the children to cook. They knew that making a box of macaroni and cheese and serving it up didn't count for dinner. They had to plan two additional items. The Rule of Three sounds simple but can be puzzling and really trip up the meal-planning; it gets easier with practice. This cookbook is designed to help with the Rule of Three when planning your menus.

Preparing Satisfying Family Dinners

As our children grew up and left home, my husband and I gradually began to eat differently, with a single protein like steak, chicken or fish, along with a vegetable on the side, often fruit for dessert. He and I don't need the dense combinations that made up our menu when I had to feed a houseful of growing boys.

Back then, if I'd served a four ounce chicken breast with a side of steamed asparagus for dinner, they would have left the table feeling starved and invaded the kitchen later, snacking to fill up. Or run out to the local fast food or pizza place, and how healthy is that?

The hearty recipes in this cookbook will provide satisfying meals for the active family at a minimum of expense and trouble. They do require preparation,

however. Although the directions are fairly simple and straightforward, my recipes don't have a lot of can-opening and processed ingredients.

To save money on food, cooking hearty dinners from pantry basics is the cheapest, most efficient way to do so. If dinner is satisfying, your family won't crave snacks as much. Sure, it would be nice if we could raise a family without having to cook for them too, but believe me, it's cheaper and less trouble in the long run to just stock that pantry, plan a weekly menu, and cook those meals.

The Picky Eater

As I've spoken to moms who would like to implement more organization into their meal-planning while saving money on groceries, the biggest obstacle seems to be the picky eater.

"My kids won't eat _____ (fill in the blank), so this won't work for me."

"My husband (or teen) doesn't like my cooking. He prefers fast food and doesn't eat dinners I prepare."

"My daughters are all on diets. They don't want to eat a big meal, afraid they'll get fat. They just pick at the food."

"My child gets full really easily. I can't get him to clean his plate."

All these complaints bring the following problems for whoever is the main cook in the household:

- Frustration as one's best laid dinner plans go awry
- Too much money spent on finding and stocking just the food everyone will eat
- Potential eating disorders as adolescents refuse to eat at mealtime then snack on junk
- Wasted ingredients that took money and time to prepare

I don't have all the answers but one thing I do know: Parents must exercise discipline and structure in family meals just as in other areas. We wouldn't let our kids forgo tooth brushing or taking their vitamins or wearing appropriate clothing for the season simply because they complained, so why should we allow it at the dinner table? I'm not in favor of force-feeding, but I believe that providing structure at meal-time will bring positive benefits in other areas as well.

These recipes will fill up younger children quickly, and they may not be able to finish a serving. I never made anyone clean their plates. When mine refused to eat what was served, I set their plate aside. Later, when they complained about being hungry, I'd tell them to go get the rest of their dinner. This usually worked, as long as I didn't cater to their whims and go fix them something different. Eating dinner shouldn't become a power play on the side of either the parent or the child.

Saving the plate out can also work for those who aren't present to eat with the family. So what if no one is home at 4 p.m.? Make dinner anyway, and when they get in, the food is ready and they should expect to eat what's prepared.

Benefits of Regular Family Meals

These methods—the Rule of Three, regularly preparing satisfying and complete family dinners, saving out the plates for those who aren't hungry or present to eat with the family—helped our children avoid weight gain during adolescence. This is the time when kids have growth spurts and crave calorie-rich foods, along with getting busier with outside activities, leading them to replace family dinner with snacks and fast food.

It may seem like too much work to prepare meals five nights a week and establish the pattern of gathering the family at dinnertime, but the benefits in physical, emotional, mental and financial health

are well worth the trouble. (I always skipped dinner prep on Friday and Saturday nights, letting the kids have their snacks and parties instead. On Sundays, we had our main meal during the day after church, with popcorn and dessert in the evenings.)

Proper weight management, balanced structure and discipline with meals, more united and happier families, less work in the long run for mom and dad, saving money on food—these are just a few of the advantages of developing the habit of cooking regular family dinners.

Keep a Supply of Basics

Menu-planning is easier with a supply of basics that can be used for multiple recipes. To make most of the recipes in this book you will need:

- Eggs, milk, butter
- Cheese: Monterey Jack, Cheddar, Parmesan
- Corn tortillas
- Fresh vegetables in season: potatoes, cabbage, onions, carrots, celery
- Fresh fruit in season: apples, oranges, grapefruit, melon, pineapple, peaches, pears, apricots
- Canned tomato soup
- Canned tomatoes and tomato sauce
- Canned pineapple, peaches, mandarin oranges, applesauce
- Dry beans: pinto, black and red, lentils
- White rice
- Soy sauce
- Garlic cloves
- Chocolate chips

- Oatmeal

- Flour, sugar, brown sugar, shortening, cocoa, vanilla, baking powder, baking soda

- Canned pumpkin

- Powdered sugar

- Raisins

- Cuts of beef, chicken and pork bought on sale and stocked in the freezer

- Bacon

- Sunflower seeds

- Sesame seeds

These are the basics for providing nutritious, inexpensive family meals. Have fun with it! Cooking doesn't have to be a tedious chore to be avoided at all costs. It's a project, a skill, a craft, a hobby, a gathering activity, a joy—and as you create your own family traditions related to food and mealtime, the shared moments will build memories to last a lifetime.

Bruce and Karen Gowen with their ten children; August, 2011.

Main Dishes

Casseroles,
Soups,
Stir-Fry,
Slow-Cooker Dishes

Chicken Broccoli Casserole

An easy way to use leftover chicken or turkey. And if you have leftover stuffing as well, you can substitute it for the prepared stuffing mix. Obviously a good choice for a post–Thanksgiving dinner.

Ingredients

3 cups chicken or turkey, cooked and cubed

1 head broccoli, cut in small pieces and steamed

2 cans cream of chicken soup

1 cup chicken broth

¾ cup mayonnaise

1 ½ teaspoon lemon juice

½ teaspoon curry powder

1 box stuffing mix, prepared

Directions

Combine soup, broth, mayonnaise, lemon juice, and curry powder for sauce. Arrange cooked chicken on bottom of 9 x 13″ baking pan. Lay cooked broccoli on top of chicken. Mix sauce and pour over chicken and broccoli. Spoon prepared stuffing over sauce. Cover with foil and bake 25 minutes at 350 degrees or until bubbly. Remove foil and bake another 10 minutes. Serves 6.

Serving suggestion: Oven-Baked Fries made with sweet potatoes (p. 33), Favorite Zucchini (p. 35), Banana Nut Cake (p. 56)

Italian Eggplant

The longest part of preparation is frying the eggplant but it can be done ahead and then the casserole baked before serving. Makes a wonderful dish for company, especially with the Home-made Egg Noodles which also can be made ahead and drying until ready to cook. This recipe can be doubled to serve 12–14.

Ingredients

One or more large eggplant, as needed (to double, I use three eggplants)

Three eggs, whisked

Italian-seasoned bread crumbs, 15 oz. can

Olive oil for frying

Mozzarella cheese, about ½ lb, grated

Your favorite spaghetti sauce, 48 oz. jar Prego recommended

Pasta noodles, such as linguini

Directions

Peel and slice eggplant. Dip slices in egg and then in bread crumbs. Deep fat fry in olive oil until golden brown. Take eggplant right from frying pan and lay out in large baking pan (11 x 14″). Grate cheese over all and pour spaghetti sauce over. Bake uncovered until bubbly at 350 degrees and serve with prepared pasta. Serves 6.

Serving suggestion: Home-made Egg Noodles (p. 49), Basil Green Beans (p. 32), Ricotta Garlic Bread (p. 47), Best Apple Crisp (p. 53)

Zucchini Sausage Bake

Another easy casserole that's rich and filling with very little preparation time. (Shown on page 32 with Greek-style Green Beans.)

Ingredients

1 lb. ground Italian sausage

5 tablespoons flour

6–8 cups sliced zucchini (about 6 medium)

One onion, chopped

1 16 oz. container cottage cheese

¼ cup grated Parmesan cheese

2 eggs, well-beaten

½ teaspoon garlic salt

1 cup (4 oz.) shredded cheddar cheese, for topping

Directions

Preheat oven to 350 degrees. In large skillet, brown sausage, breaking into small pieces. Remove from pan and spread on bottom of 11 x 7″ baking pan. Sprinkle the meat with one tablespoon of the flour and stir around. In same skillet, cook zucchini and onion until tender but not brown. Remove from heat. Toss with remaining flour (4 tablespoons). Spoon half the zucchini mixture over meat.

In medium bowl, mix cottage cheese, grated Parmesan, eggs and garlic salt. (Reserve the shredded cheddar cheese.) Spoon cheese mixture evenly over zucchini layer and top with remaining zucchini. Bake 30–40 minutes at 350 degrees, covered. Top with cheddar cheese and bake, uncovered, five minutes longer. Serves 10.

Serving suggestions: Super Hero Spinach Salad (p. 28), Coconut Cream Cake (p. 57)

Sausage Egg Casserole

This makes an excellent brunch item—or fun when you want to switch things up and have breakfast for dinner.

Ingredients

4 boiled eggs

¼ cup margarine or butter

¼ cup flour

2 cups milk

½ lb. ground sausage

2 cans corn, drained

½ cup bread crumbs

½ teaspoon salt

Directions

Preheat oven to 375 degrees. Slice two of the eggs into a 1½-quart casserole dish and set aside. Cook sausage; pour off fat and set aside.

In saucepan, melt butter then blend in the flour, salt and dash of pepper. Add milk all at once and stir rapidly with a whisk to break up any lumps. Continue to cook, stirring constantly until mixture thickens and bubbles. Remove from heat and stir sausage and corn into sauce; pour over sliced eggs in casserole dish.

Slice remaining two eggs and arrange on top of the mixture. Sprinkle with the bread crumbs. Bake at 375 degrees for 30–35 minutes or until bubbly. Serves 4–6.

Serving suggestion: Scottish Oat Scones (p. 45), Fancy Fruit Salad (p. 30)

Chalupas

Another crowd-pleasing, easy to make casserole; like enchiladas only not. Something different, not real spicy.

Ingredients

2 cups chopped onions

2 cups water

½ cup flour

1/3 cup chili powder

2 lbs. ground beef

3 cans tomato soup

2 cans evaporated milk

24 corn tortillas

4 cups grated cheddar cheese

Directions

Saute half the onions in meat until browned. Add flour and chili powder; cook for five minutes. Add water. Cover, simmer until thick. Mix canned soup, milk, and remaining onions. Add to meat mixture. Layer tortillas, meat mixture and cheese in 11 x 14″ baking dish until all ingredients are used up, ending with the cheese. Bake at 325 until bubbly, about an hour. Serves 10.

Serving suggestion: Broccoli Salad (p. 29), Steamed White Rice (p. 41), Family Flan (p. 62)

Hamburger Tamale Pie

One of my favorite ways of making a pound of ground beef feed a family of ten

Ingredients

1 lb. hamburger meat

1 medium to large yellow onion, chopped

Garlic clove, chopped

1 can (16 oz.) tomatoes

1 can (16 oz.) whole kernel corn, drained

20–24 pitted black olives

2 tablespoons chili powder

1½ teaspoon salt

1 cup cornmeal

1 cup milk

2 eggs, beaten

1 cup shredded cheddar cheese (4 oz.)

Directions

Preheat oven to 350 degrees. Cook and stir meat, onion and garlic until meat is brown; drain. Stir in tomatoes with liquid, corn, olives, chili powder and salt. Heat to boiling, breaking up tomatoes. Pour into ungreased baking dish, 9 x 11″, or 2-quart casserole dish.

Mix cornmeal, milk and eggs. Pour over meat mixture. Sprinkle with cheese. Bake in 350-degree oven until golden brown, about 40–50 minutes. Serves 8.

Variation: If you prefer a thick tamale crust, double the cornmeal, milk, eggs and cheese.

Serving suggestion: Stir-fried Cabbage with Bacon (p. 31), Deliciously Decadent Brownies (p. 60)

Cheesy Easy Lasagna

Except for cooking the lasagna noodles and browning the ground beef, there's not much to this recipe beyond layering the ingredients and baking!

Ingredients

3 cups ricotta cheese

3 cups shredded mozzarella cheese

2 eggs

2 lb. ground beef

1 large jar (67 oz.) traditional spaghetti sauce, about 8 cups

18–20 lasagna noodles, cooked al dente and drained

2–3 cups grated Parmesan cheese, enough to cover top of lasagna

Directions

Mix ricotta, mozzarella and eggs. Set aside. Brown ground beef, stirring to separate. Pour off fat. Stir in spaghetti sauce. Cook lasagna noodles, drain and rinse in cold water. Layer meat/sauce mixture, then noodles, then cheese.. Repeat as needed. Top with remaining noodles, remaining sauce and Parmesan cheese.

Bake at 400 degrees for 30–45 minutes, until lasagna is bubbly. Let stand ten minutes before cutting. Serves 12.

Serving suggestions: Spinach Orange Salad (p. 28), Amber Pie (p. 64)

Cheese and Olive Casserole/Oven Pizza

A do-ahead dish for weekend brunch or for next-day dinner on a busy day, this one's a favorite with cheese-lovers.

Ingredients

8 slices white bread

½ lb. Monterey jack cheese, shredded

½ lb. sharp cheddar cheese, shredded

6 eggs

4 cups milk

1–2 cups sliced ripe olives

Green olives stuffed with pimento for garnish

Directions

Butter a 9 x 13″ baking pan. Alternate layers of bread, cheeses, and ripe olives. Beat eggs and combine with milk. Pour over bread/cheese layers.

Refrigerate for at least an hour, or overnight. Bake in a 350-degree oven for one hour. Before serving, scatter the green olives around the top. Serves 6.

Serving suggestion: Seven Layer Salad (p. 30), Fruit and Nut Muffins (p. 42)

Variations: Add a package of pepperoni and substitute mozzarella cheese to make Oven Pizza.

Meatless Enchilada Casserole

Ingredients

18 corn tortillas

1 lb. Monterey jack cheese, cut into strips

3 small cans green chilies

½ cup butter

3 cups sour cream

2 cups cottage cheese

1 can (10 oz.) enchilada sauce

Salt and pepper to taste

Directions

Preheat oven to 350 degrees. Mix sour cream and cottage cheese and season to taste with salt and pepper. Saute tortillas in butter for about thirty seconds on each side. Spread two tablespoons of sour cream mixture over sautéed tortillas. Place several strips of cheese and a few chilies on top of mixture and roll.

Place rolled tortillas close together in shallow baking pan. Spoon any remaining sour cream mixture, strips of cheese and chilies on top of the rolled tortillas. Pour enchilada sauce over all and bake, uncovered, for 25 minutes or until heated through. Serves 6.

Serving suggestion: Broccoli Salad (p. 29), Orange Spice Cake (p. 59)

Enchilawesome

My family loves enchiladas. Our kids could have eaten them every night. This recipe includes the enchilada sauce recipe, but to save time you can use the prepared, canned enchilada sauce. You will need about four cups of enchilada sauce.

Ingredients

16 oz. bag corn chips, such as Fritos

1 lb. ground beef

1 large can enchilada sauce (or make your own, recipe follows)

1 cup fresh Anaheim peppers, diced

1½ teaspoon salt

1 medium to large yellow onion, chopped

1 lb. grated cheddar cheese

Directions

Prepare enchilada sauce if you plan on making your own.

In skillet, brown ground beef, then drain off fat. Add enchilada sauce, diced peppers, onion, and salt. Simmer for fifteen minutes on low heat.

Preheat oven to 350 degrees. In 9 x 12″ baking pan, place one layer of corn chips. Spoon a layer of meat sauce over. Sprinkle with grated cheese. Repeat. Add more enchilada sauce if mixture seems too dry. Bake for 20 minutes at 350 degrees. Serves 6.

Serving suggestion: Favorite Zucchini (p. 35), Steamed White Rice (p. 41)

Enchilada Sauce

Ingredients

2 cups tomato sauce

2 cups water

4 teaspoons dried onion powder

2 beef bouillon cubes

½ teaspoon salt

½ teaspoon garlic powder

1 teaspoon chili powder

Directions

Mix ingredients in sauce pan. Simmer for 5 minutes. Makes one quart.

Beef and Egg on Rice

This is a traditional Japanese dish that is somewhat like stir fry, somewhat like soup. It is satisfying, easy to make and something a little different from the usual stir fry.

Ingredients

8 ounces sirloin steak, cut into thin strips

1 teaspoon plus 2 tablespoons soy sauce

2 tablespoons mirin, or any sweet Oriental sauce

⅛ teaspoon black pepper

2 cups water

1 medium yellow onion, cut into thin wedges

8 green onion and tops, cut diagonally into ½ inch lengths

3 large eggs, lightly beaten

3–6 cups hot cooked rice

Directions

Slice beef as directed and place on a plate; add 1 teaspoon soy sauce. "In a bowl, combine remaining 2 tablespoons soy sauce, mirin, pepper and 2 cups water; set aside. Heat large frying pan or wok over high heat. Lightly coat inside of pan with cooking spray. Add beef and stir-fry two minutes or until lightly browned. Remove from pan. Lightly coat inside of same pan with additional cooking spray. Add yellow onion slices and stir-fry until just barely tender, about two or three minutes. Add soy-mirin mixture. Bring to a boil. Mix in green onions with tops and the beef. Add eggs; *do not stir*. Reduce heat and simmer uncovered until egg is cooked. Remove from heat.

Spoon cooked rice into shallow soup bowls. Top each with equal portions of beef mixture, including liquid. Makes 4 servings, using ¾ cup cooked rice and one cup beef mixture each.

Serving suggestion: Spinach Orange Salad (p. 28), Butterscotch Dumplings (p. 62)

Red Beans and Rice

Ingredients

1 lb. dried red beans

1 lb. ground sausage

2 cups chopped onion

2 green peppers, chopped

½ cup snipped fresh parsley

1 (8 oz.) can tomato sauce

Several cloves garlic, minced

1 tablespoon salt

½ teaspoon black pepper

¼ teaspoon dried oregano

Massachusetts Clam Chowder

Since this recipe was given to me by a Massachusetts native, I consider it legitimately regional. The fact that it's easy to make is an added bonus.

Ingredients

4 cans baby clams

2 mediumonions, finely chopped

½ stick (¼ cup) real butter

6–8 large potatoes, peeled and cubed

1 teaspoon salt

4 cups whole milk

¼ teaspoon dried thyme

Few dashes bottled hot pepper sauce

6 cups hot cooked rice

Directions

Rinse the beans and place them in a large pot. Add eight cups cold water. Bring to a boil; reduce heat and simmer for two minutes. Remove from heat. Cover and let stand for one hour, then drain and rinse. (This method works well for cooking dry beans for any recipe.)

Return beans to pot. Add more than enough water to cover beans. Cover pot and simmer until beans are barely tender, about an hour. Meanwhile, brown sausage with chopped onions, green peppers and garlic. Drain well. Add the meat and vegetable mixture along with the parsley, tomato sauce and seasonings to the pot of beans. Bring mixture to a boil; reduce heat and simmer, covered, over low heat for about an hour.

Serve on plates over hot cooked white rice, with bottled hot pepper sauce for those who want to spice it up. Serves 10.

Serving suggestion: Poppy Seed Loaf (p. 39), Seven Layer Salad (p. 30), Coconut Lime Squares (p. 53)

Directions

Melt butter in large saucepan. Add chopped onions and sauté. Let simmer 3–5 minutes until onions are transparent, then add 3 cans of baby clams, including juice. Simmer 5 minutes. Add cubed potatoes, salt and enough water to cover. Simmer until potatoes are soft. With a spoon, mash about half the potatoes against side of pan. Stir.

Add milk and the fourth can of clams. *Do not boil!* Season to taste with salt and pepper. Serves 8.

Serving suggestions: Maine Muffins (p. 42), Fancy Fruit Salad (p. 30)

Spicy Black Bean Soup

Having a variety of recipes that use dry beans in creative ways is one of the best ways to save money on food. Eating beans doesn't have to mean opening a can and feeling deprived. Although this list

of ingredients may appear daunting, they're fairly basic items you should already have in your pantry or easily found at the store. Preparation is simple, consisting of putting everything together in a large pot. I make this soup when I have a large ham bone left from a bone-in ham, purchased when they go on sale.

Ingredients

2 lb. dried black beans, cleaned and sorted

4 quarts water

4 slices bacon, cut into small pieces

3 cups diced onion

¼ cup chopped garlic

Large ham bone

4 quarts chicken stock
     (if you don't have chicken stock, use 4 qts. water
     and 12 chicken bouillon cubes)

2 tablespoons ground cumin

2 teaspoons oregano

2 teaspoons salt

2 teaspoons black pepper

3 tablespoons chopped parsley

3 tablespoons chopped cilantro

1 teaspoon cayenne pepper

1 bay leaf

1 cup diced red pepper

3 Anaheim peppers, seeded and diced

¼ cup brown sugar

Juice from half a lime, freshly squeezed

Sour cream, optional

Directions

Rinse black beans thoroughly and put in large pot with 4 quarts water. Bring to boil then let set for one hour. Drain. Return beans to pot. Meanwhile, sauté onion and garlic with the bacon until tender. Bacon does not need to be crisp.

Add the bacon, onions and garlic, along with ham bone and chicken stock to the pot. Stir in the spices: cumin, oregano, bay leaf, salt, black pepper, cayenne, parsley and cilantro. Bring to a boil, then reduce heat, cover and simmer for six hours, or until beans are tender and ham falls off the bone.

Remove ham bone. Pull off and shred any remaining meat and return to pot. Add the chopped red pepper and Anaheim, brown sugar and lime juice. Simmer another hour. Serve topped with Salsa Fresca and sour cream. Serves 10.

Serving suggestions: Mom's Cornbread (p. 45), Salsa Fresca (p. 29)

Thick Lentil Soup

Ingredients

3–4 slices bacon

2 medium onions, sliced

3 large carrots, peeled and sliced

2 large stalks celery, chopped

4 cloves garlic, diced

4 cups water

2 cups (12 oz. bag) dried lentils

2 chicken bouillon cubes

3 tablespoons snipped fresh parsley

1 tablespoon salt

½ teaspoon black pepper

1 teaspoon thyme

1 bay leaf

1 can (28 oz.) whole tomatoes

1 cup water

Directions

Fry bacon in 3-quart saucepan or Dutch oven until just crisp; drain on paper towel. Add onion, carrot, celery and garlic to bacon fat in pan. Cook and stir over medium heat until celery is tender, about ten minutes. Break bacon into pieces and add to pan. Stir in four cups water, the lentils, bouillon, parsley, salt, pepper, thyme and bay leaf. Heat to boiling; reduce heat. Cover and simmer until lentils soften, about an hour.

Add tomatoes with their liquid and one cup water. Cover and simmer an additional thirty minutes, or until soup thickens. Add more water as necessary. Serves 8.

Serving suggestion: Buttery Biscuit Sticks (p. 39), Cinnamon Apples (p. 53)

Flu-Busting Chicken Soup

Fall and winter is when a big pot of chicken soup helps everyone feel better, whether you're in the early stages of catching cold or just need warming up!

Ingredients

One chicken, whole or cut in pieces

2 fresh jalapeño peppers

3 or 4 whole garlic cloves

1 tablespoon salt

2 onions, peeled and diced

4 carrots, peeled and chopped

4 stalks celery, chopped, reserve the leaves for stock

chopped garlic to taste (I like to use 6–8 for flu-busting soup)

herbs and seasonings to taste:
  parsley, tarragon, basil, oregano, sage

4 cups canned crushed tomatoes

1 cup uncooked rice or barley

Directions

Cover chicken with water in a large stock pot. Add celery leaves, unchopped, the whole jalapeño peppers, 3 or 4 garlic cloves, and salt. Bring to a boil and simmer for an hour, or until chicken is cooked through but not falling off the bone.

Remove from heat and allow to cool to room temperature. Remove chicken, garlic cloves and celery leaves to a large bowl. Skim fat off top of chicken stock.

Take meat off bones and save. Chop remaining vegetables and add to stock. With a spoon, break up the softened jalapeño peppers. Bring soup to a boil and simmer until carrots are tender, about an hour. Add uncooked rice and simmer another thirty minutes. Add chicken and heat through.

Makes a large pot that isn't as spicy as one might think, considering the jalapeños. If you want less kick to it, use only one but remember it's the peppers that contribute to its healing qualities.

Serving suggestion: Herb Dumplings (p. 48), Mom's Cornbread (p. 45)

Boiled Dinner

My grandmother Julia Marker taught me how to make this when I was a girl. I enjoyed it then and still do. I've made it without the beef, just the vegetables, but my boys prefer it with meat. Otherwise it barely fills them up.

Ingredients

5 lbs. potatoes, peeled

3 large onions, peeled and cut in half

4–6 turnips, peeled and cut in half

1 head cabbage, quartered

2–3 lb. chuck roast

1 tablespoon salt

½ teaspoon pepper

Directions

Brown meat in 1 tablespoon oil in large stock pan. Add 2 quarts water, salt, and bring to a boil. Cover, lower heat and simmer until meat is tender. Add potatoes, peeled and whole; turnips and onions, either whole or cut in half. Add enough water to cover vegetables and simmer until potatoes are tender. Add cabbage, along with more water if necessary. Simmer until cabbage is cooked and meat is falling apart. Break it into pieces then cook an additional fifteen minutes to blend flavors. Add more salt and pepper to taste.

Serving suggestions: Refrigerator Rolls (p. 49), Banana Nut Cake (p. 56)

Basic Home-made Chili

I vary my chili recipe every time I make it, just can't help myself. Sometimes I add vegetables like green or red peppers, chopped zucchini, jalapeño or Anaheim peppers, leftover soup or meat, basically whatever is on hand that I think will add to the flavor and texture, or to use up bits of this or that in the fridge.

Ingredients

1 lb. package dry pinto beans

1 or 2 lbs. ground beef

2 (14.5 oz.) cans diced tomatoes

1 large onion, chopped

5 cloves garlic, diced

3 stalks celery, chopped

2½ teaspoons salt

3 tablespoons chili powder, or to taste

1 tablespoon cumin

Directions

Rinse and cook beans. Cook until tender, *without salt,* in plenty of water, for about one and a half hours. Brown meat in large skillet. Add chopped onion, garlic and celery. Stir well and simmer until onion is translucent. Drain off fat. Add one teaspoon salt to meat/vegetable mixture and set aside.

When beans are tender, drain and reserve water. Add meat/vegetable mixture to pot of beans. Add tomatoes, 1½ teaspoon salt and the chili powder and cumin to taste. Simmer one to three hours, adding bean-cooking liquid as needed. Mash part of beans against side of pan with spoon. This thickens the chili.

Serving suggestion: Buttermilk Biscuits (p. 41), Family Flan (p. 62)

Quick Ginger Chicken

Oriental dishes can be easy to do and a painless way to stretch protein and include more vegetables in the diet.

Ingredients

⅓ cup water

3 tablespoons soy sauce

1 tablespoon cornstarch

1 teaspoon sugar

1½ teaspoon minced ginger or ½ teaspoon dried ginger

3 tablespoons oil, divided

2 red or green peppers, cut into strips

6 green onions, cut into 2-inch pieces

1 large clove garlic, minced

2 large chicken breasts, skinned, boned and cut into 1-inch chunks

Directions

Stir water, soy sauce, cornstarch, sugar and ginger until smooth; set aside. In wok or large frying pan, heat one tablespoon oil over medium high heat. Add peppers, green onions and garlic; sauté four minutes. Remove. Add remaining oil, heat; add chicken, sauté until lightly browned. Stir cornstarch mixture and add to skillet with vegetables, stirring constantly. Bring to boil over medium heat; boil one minute. Serve over rice or noodles. Serves 4.

Serving suggestion: Steamed White Rice (p. 41), Eggnog Muffins (p. 43), Pineapple Upside Down Cake (p. 55)

Green Pepper Steak

A simple stir-fry that uses an inexpensive cut of beef and a variety of fresh vegetables.

Ingredients

1 lb. beef chuck or round, fat trimmed

¼ cup soy sauce

1 clove garlic

1½ teaspoon grated fresh ginger or ½ teaspoon ground ginger

¼ cup oil

1 cup green onion, thinly sliced

1 cup green or red peppers, cut into 1-inch squares

2 stalks celery, thickly sliced on the diagonal

1 tablespoon cornstarch

1 cup water

2 tomatoes, cut into wedges

Directions

With a very sharp knife, cut beef across grain into thin strips ⅛ inches thick. In a bowl, combine soy sauce, garlic, ginger; add beef. Toss and set aside while preparing vegetables.

Heat oil in wok or large fry pan. Add beef and toss over high heat until browned. Taste meat for tenderness. If not tender, cover pan and simmer meat for thirty or forty minutes over very low heat. Watch carefully so it doesn't burn. Add a tablespoon of water as needed.

Turn up heat and add vegetables. Cook until tender but crisp, about eight to ten minutes. Mix cornstarch with water. Add to pan, stir and cook until thickened. Add tomatoes and heat through. Makes four servings. To serve eight, double the ingredients but reduce water to 1¾ cup. Add another ½ tablespoon cornstarch to doubled amount.

Serving suggestion: Steamed White Rice, Nonfat Pumpkin Bread

Beef and Broccoli Stir Fry

By now you may have guessed that stir fry is a favorite of mine; it stretches the meat and painlessly inserts vegetables into the meal.

Ingredients

2 large stalks broccoli

1 lb. beef top round, or other cut such as sirloin or chuck steak

¼ cup oil

1 can (20 oz.) pineapple chunks, in syrup

¼ cup soy sauce

2 tablespoons vinegar

½ teaspoon crushed red pepper (use less for less spicy)

2 tablespoons cornstarch

1 cup fresh bean sprouts

1 tablespoon sesame seeds

Directions

Trim and slice broccoli diagonally. Slice beef in thin strips across the grain. Heat oil in wok or large skillet until very hot. Add broccoli and stir fry two or three minutes until barely tender. Add beef strips and cook just until brown. Remove pan from heat.

Drain pineapple, reserving syrup. Mix syrup with soy sauce, vinegar, red pepper and cornstarch. Add pineapple, bean sprouts and sauce mixture to beef and broccoli in pan. Heat and stir until thickened. Sprinkle with sesame seeds. Serve over rice or noodles. Makes four large servings; double for more.

Serving suggestion: Home-made Egg Noodles (p. 49), Lemonade Cake (p. 58)

Slow Cooker Boneless Pork Ribs

A tangy, tender meat dish that slow cooks all day

Ingredients

3–4 lbs. boneless pork ribs, country style

2 tablespoons oil

One onion, finely chopped

2 cups catsup

¼ cup soy sauce

4 garlic cloves, minced

2 teaspoons mustard

2 teaspoons paprika

1 teaspoon salt

½ teaspoon pepper

1 teaspoon seasoned salt

1 teaspoon granulated garlic, garlic salt, or garlic powder

2 tablespoons brown sugar

Directions

Combine sauce ingredients in slow cooker. Brown ribs in two tablespoons oil in skillet, turning to brown completely. Remove ribs from skillet and transfer to slow cooker.

Cover and cook on low all day, for 6–8 hours, or until tender. Serves 8.

Serving suggestion: Irish Potatoes (p. 35), Salad in a Bag (p. 29), Buttery Biscuit Sticks (p. 39)

Cajun Pot Roast

Chuck roast is a less expensive cut of beef that does well when cooked long for tenderness. I like to watch the sales and buy several for the freezer.

Ingredients

1 3–4 lb. boneless beef chuck roast

2–3 teaspoons Cajun seasoning

1 tablespoon oil

2 cans (14.5 oz.) diced or stewed tomatoes

1 onion, chopped

1 cup chopped celery

2 cloves garlic, minced, or 1 teaspoon prepared, chopped garlic or ½ teaspoon granulated, dried garlic

¼ cup quick-cooking tapioca

To make your own Cajun seasoning, mix together: 1–1½ teaspoon seasoning salt, ½–¾ teaspoon ground red pepper (cayenne), and ½–¾ teaspoon ground black pepper.

Directions

Trim fat from roast. Cut meat if necessary to fit in slow cooker. Rub Cajun seasoning all over. In a large skillet, brown roast on all sides in hot oil.

In slow cooker, combine undrained tomatoes, onion, celery, tapioca, and garlic. Place meat on top of vegetable mixture. Cover and cook on low heat setting for 10–12 hours or on high heat setting for 5–6 hours. Serve meat with sauce on a bed of rice or noodles. Serves 6.

Variation: Add additional vegetables, like sliced mushrooms, bell peppers, jalapeño or Anaheim pepper if you want it spicier; instead of tapioca, blend ½ cup cornstarch or flour in one cup of water and add to slow cooker with vegetables.

Serving suggestion: Oven-baked Fries (p. 33), Salad in a Bag (p. 29), Famous Texas Cake (p. 58)

Pulled Pork Barbecue

This is ideal for a large gathering.

Ingredients

2 onions, sliced

2–5 lb. pork roast

5–6 whole cloves

2 cups water

2 or 3 bottles (16 oz.) bbq sauce

1 large onion, chopped

Directions

Place one sliced onion in bottom of slow cooker. Add meat, cloves, and water, with second sliced onion on top of meat. Cover and cook on low for 8–12 hours. (I like to start it overnight.)

In the morning, pull meat from slow cooker onto a large pan. Remove bone and fat then return meat to cooker. Add chopped onion and two bottles bbq sauce. Cover and cook an additional two or three hours on high, stirring only occasionally. Add additional bbq sauce as needed. Turn to low if it will be awhile before you need it.

Serve from pot on hamburger buns. Makes 12–16 sandwiches.

Serving suggestion: Fancy Fruit Salad (p. 30), Orange Spice Cake (p. 59)

Slow Cooker Beef Stew

I appreciate my slow cooker for ease and convenience, as long as I remember to get the ingredients in soon enough. If your slow-cooker isn't large enough for this recipe, it can be put in a covered roasting pan and baked in the oven all day at 250 degrees. The added peas and corn at the end make it colorful and appetizing. This recipe makes a lot!

Ingredients

4 lb. chuck roast

2 tablespoons oil

½ cup flour

1 tablespoon salt

4 cups water

8 medium potatoes, peeled and chopped

6–8 carrots, peeled and sliced

1 large onion, halved and quartered

½ teaspoon garlic powder

⅛ teaspoon black pepper

1 16 oz. bag frozen peas

1 16 oz. bag frozen corn

½ cup additional flour

2 cups water

Directions

Cut roast into bite-sized chunks, removing fat and gristle, and place in a large bowl. Add one-half cup of the flour and stir until beef chunks are coated with the flour. Heat two tablespoons oil in frying pan; brown meat in oil, stirring frequently.

Place browned beef in slow cooker, sprinkle with tablespoon of salt, cover and set on low while preparing the vegetables. Add the chopped potatoes, carrots, onion, garlic powder and pepper to slow cooker, along with four cups of water. Cook on high for 6–8 hours, stirring well after three hours.

One hour before serving, stir in the frozen peas and corn. (If your slow cooker is already full, this is where you need to move the stew to a large covered roasting pan and cook the rest of the time in a 325-degree oven. Or take out a portion of stew, add the peas, corn and remaining ingredients; continue cooking until done. Before serving, stir in the extra portion.)

After adding the peas and corn to stew, measure two cups water into a bowl. Stir one-half cup flour gradually to the water and then whisk rapidly to make a paste. Add flour/water mixture back to slow cooker and stir well. Continue cooking on high until stew is thickened and the peas and corn are cooked through. Makes one very large pot of stew. Serves 10–12.

Serving suggestion: Refrigerator Rolls (p. 49), Easy Chocolate Cake (p. 59)

Salads and Vegetables

Far Out Salad

Main dish salads are wonderful for summer-time lunches. This one uses left-over cooked chicken and other inexpensive, basic ingredients.

Ingredients

½ cup rice vinegar

1 tablespoon soy sauce

1 teaspoon ground ginger

1 cup cooked chicken, chopped

4 cups raw cabbage, shredded

1 carrot, peeled and shredded

2 green onions, sliced

2 tablespoons sesame seeds, toasted

Directions

Combine vinegar, soy sauce and ginger. Add chicken and marinate for fifteen to thirty minutes. In salad bowl, combine remaining ingredients. Just before serving, remove chicken from marinade. Pour marinade into cabbage mixture and toss. Top with chicken and serve. Serves 4–6.

Serving suggestion: Scottish Oat Scones (p. 45), Coconut Lime Squares (p. 55)

Oriental Chicken Salad

A bit more elaborate than the previous chicken salad, this is a heavier salad, makes more, and always gets requests to share the recipe.

Ingredients

1 head raw cabbage, chopped

6 green onions, chopped

4–6 chicken breasts, cooked and diced

2 packages uncooked Ramen noodles, any flavor

4 tablespoons sliced almonds

4 tablespoons sesame seeds

Directions

Preheat oven to 400 degrees. Break up the Ramen noodles and combine with almonds and sesame seeds. Place on a cookie sheet and toast lightly in oven for three to four minutes, but watch closely as they burn easily. Remove from oven and set aside. Combine the cabbage, onions and chicken. Add the noodles, almonds and sesame seed mixture to salad. Toss to combine. Pour Oriental Salad Dressing (recipe follows) over salad before serving; toss well to completely coat. Serves 6–8.

Serving suggestion: Fruit and Nut Muffins (p. 42), Pineapple Upside Down Cake (p. 55) with vanilla ice cream

Oriental Salad Dressing

Ingredients

3–4 tablespoons sugar

1 teaspoon salt

1 teaspoon pepper

3 teaspoons soy sauce

2 tablespoons white vinegar

2 flavor packets from the Ramen noodles

1 cup vegetable oil

Directions

Combine all ingredients except oil and stir well until sugar is dissolved. Add oil and shake well.

Spinach Orange Salad

Ingredients

1 lb. fresh spinach

2 (11 oz.) can mandarin oranges, drained

1 medium purple onion, thickly sliced and separated into rings

Directions

Remove stems from spinach, wash leaves, pat dry. Tear leaves into bite-sized pieces. Combine spinach, oranges and onions. Toss with Tangy Orange Vinaigrette Dressing just before serving.

Tangy Orange Vinaigrette Dressing

Ingredients

1½ tablespoon grated orange rind

1½ tablespoon Dijon mustard

½ teaspoon minced garlic

½ teaspoon salt

¼ teaspoon hot sauce

¼ cup cider vinegar

½ cup vegetable oil

Directions

Using blender, combine first five ingredients and pulse until well-blended. Add oil and mix until well-blended. Pour over salad and serve immediately.

Serving suggestion: Grilled meat or chicken, Herb-roasted Potatoes (p. 34)

Super Hero Spinach Salad

When you want something special for company, or to take to a pot-luck, without having to go to a whole lot of trouble.

Ingredients

1 large bag fresh spinach leaves, (about 2.5 lb. total)

1 bag 3-bean mix sprouts (about 8 oz.)

½ cup raw sunflower seeds

8 eggs, hard-boiled

1 red onion, thinly sliced

1 lb. package sliced mushrooms

As desired: croutons, shredded carrot, sliced radish

Restaurant-style Italian dressing of high quality, such as Paul Newman's

Directions

Combine all ingredients except dressing and croutons, to have on the side. Serves 10–12.

Serving Suggestion: Oven Pizza (p. 13), Cinnamon Apples (p. 53)

Salad in a Bag

Ingredients

6 tablespoons olive oil

6 tablespoons red wine vinegar

2 teaspoon basil

2 teaspoon oregano

Salt and freshly ground black pepper to taste

2 sweet red peppers, seeded and cut into thin strips

2 green peppers, seeded and cut into thin strips

1 Bermuda onion, thinly sliced

Directions

Whisk together olive oil, vinegar, basil, oregano and salt and pepper. Pour into a gallon-sized zipper seal bag. Add peppers and onions. Seal bag, toss up and down, and let stand at room temperature until ready to serve. Pour into serving bowl, squeezing out all dressing. Serves 6.

Salsa Fresca

Ingredients

8 medium, ripe tomatoes

1 onion

½ cup cilantro

8 cloves garlic

½ cup lime juice

4 fresh jalapeños

1 teaspoon salt

1 (16 oz.) cans tomato sauce

Directions

Chop tomatoes, onion and garlic and add to large bowl. Cover in lime juice, sprinkle with salt. Wearing gloves, prepare jalapeños. Slice length-wise, remove seeds and rinse jalapeños. Dice and add to tomato mixture. Add in seeds to taste (the seeds make it hot). For mild salsa, add the seeds of one-half jalapeño; for moderate, add seeds from two peppers; for hot, from three peppers; for very hot, from all four.

Chop cilantro and add. May add more than ½ cup if you like a stronger cilantro flavor. Add the tomato sauce and mix well. Refrigerate for several hours or overnight before serving. Makes 2–3 quarts.

Variations

For Black Bean Salsa—Cook 1-lb. package of dried black beans according to package directions. Drain and rinse well; add to salsa.

For Shrimp Ceviche—To salsa, add 4 cucumbers peeled and chopped, and ½ lb. or more cooked, deveined, chopped shrimp. Serve on tostadas.

Broccoli Salad

A great way to get your family to eat their vegetables. Even when they were little, my kids loved this salad, probably because of the bacon.

Ingredients

6 cups broccoli flowerets, cut into small, bite-sized pieces

¼ cup sunflower seeds

1 cup raisins

6 green onions, chopped

1 cup mayonnaise, or as needed

1 tablespoon sugar

1 tablespoon vinegar

12 oz. package bacon, fried crisp and crumbled

Directions

Toss broccoli, seeds, raisins and green onions in salad bowl. Combine the dressing ingredients in a separate bowl. Stir well and add to broccoli mixture. Add bacon, mix well and serve. Best when served immediately although it's good leftover too. Serves 6–8.

Serving suggestion: Slow Cooker Boneless Pork Ribs (p. 20), Famous Texas Cake (p. 58)

Seven Layer Salad

This is one of my favorite ways to use up random vegetables in the fridge. The ones given are the first choice, but you can add any others to the layers and it's just as good. Then you top with mayonnaise and serve. Leftovers don't go soggy since the mayonnaise stays on top even after refrigerating.

Ingredients

Iceberg lettuce, broken into bite-sized pieces

Celery, diced

Onion, any kind, diced, enough to make a thin layer

Grated cheddar cheese, enough to cover one layer

Frozen green peas, thawed

Imitation bacon bits

Good quality mayonnaise, Best Foods recommended

Directions

In a pan, sized 9 x 13″ or larger, depending on how many you are serving, layer each ingredient in order given, ending with another layer of lettuce. Top with the mayonnaise, enough to cover the lettuce as much as possible. Refrigerate until ready to serve. If there are leftovers, don't blend the salad or put into a different container, but cover with layers as intact as possible and refrigerate. It will be good for a day or two after.

Serving suggestion: Herb-roasted Potatoes (p. 34), Roasted Garlic (p. 34)

Fancy Fruit Salad

This is my go-to side dish when I entertain at a family event, like a mission farewell or reception. It can be doubled or tripled to serve dozens of people, chilled until ready to serve.

Ingredients

2⅗ oz. packages instant pudding, coconut cream or pistachio

1 20 oz. can pineapple tidbits, in its own juice, undrained

1 20 oz. can crushed pineapple, in its own juice

2 11 oz. cans mandarin oranges, drained

½ cup flaked coconut

4 cups red or green seedless grapes

2 cups miniature marshmallows

1 16 oz. carton frozen whipped topping, thawed

Directions

In a large bowl, mix instant pudding mix with crushed pineapple and pineapple tidbits and their juices. Let stand five minutes and then stir in remaining ingredients. Blend well. Pour into a large serving bowl (I like to use a glass punch bowl). Cover and refrigerate until ready to serve. Chill for at least two hours. Serves 15–20.

Golden Squash Bake

A wonderful supper to have when summer squash is plentiful. Zucchini can be substituted for the crook-neck squash.

Ingredients

2 lb. yellow crookneck squash, or about 8 cups sliced

4 eggs, separated

2 cups cottage cheese

4 tablespoons flour

1½ teaspoon salt

2 cup (8 oz.) shredded cheddar cheese

1 lb. bacon, cooked crisp and crumbled

Directions

Preheat oven to 350 degrees. In covered saucepan, cook sliced squash in small amount of salted water until tender, about five minutes. (If using frozen

sliced squash, simply allow to thaw. No need to cook.) Drain. In medium bowl, combine egg yolks, cottage cheese, flour and salt. Beat egg whites until stiff; fold into cottage cheese mixture.

In greased 11 x 7″ baking dish, layer half the squash, half the egg mixture, half the cheddar cheese and half the bacon. Repeat layering once more, using up all the ingredients. Bake for 20–25 minutes at 350 degrees. Serves 8.

Serving suggestion: Maine Muffins (p. 42), Seven Layer Salad (p. 30)

Stir-fried Cabbage with Bacon

When you're at the end of the monthly food budget but still want to eat well. And a reason to buy bacon on sale and keep it in the freezer. This can be used as a side dish or a main meal; just add rice.

Ingredients

3 slices smoked bacon

4 cloves garlic, minced

1 large onion, chopped

1 large head cabbage, cut into ½-inch wedges and then chopped

1 large carrot, peeled and grated

Salt and pepper to taste

Directions

Cut the bacon into ½-inch strips. Cook slowly in a large pot over low heat until the strips are cooked but not crisp. Add the garlic and onion to the bacon and sauté in the bacon grease. After a few minutes add the grated carrot and stir slightly. Add the sliced,

chopped cabbage to the pot. Stir, cover and simmer over low heat until cabbage is completely wilted. Add salt and pepper to taste and serve.

Serving suggestion: As a main meal, serve with Steamed White Rice (p. 41) and Nutty Muffins (p. 43).

Basil Green Beans

Ingredients

2 (16 oz.) packages frozen green beans

1 can Italian-style stewed tomatoes

3 cloves fresh garlic, chopped

2 tablespooons olive oil

¼ cup fresh basil, or 2 tablespoons dried

Salt and pepper to taste

Directions

Saute chopped garlic in oil until lightly browned. Add frozen green beans and stir fry until lightly done, not limp. Drain can of Italian stewed tomatoes, reserving juice. Add tomatoes to green beans, stir and break up tomatoes with spoon. Season with salt, pepper and basil. Add remaining juice from can, stir until heated through and serve. Serves 6.

Serving suggestion: Slow Cooker Boneless Pork Ribs (p. 20), Irish Potatoes (p. 35), Overnight Coffee Cake (p. 43)

Greek-style Green Beans

Ingredients

2 cups onions, diced

2 tablespoons vegetable oil

½ cube (¼ cup) butter

1 (28 oz.) can diced tomatoes; or five whole fresh tomatoes, diced

2 (14.5 oz.) cans green beans, drained, or 2 lbs. fresh or frozen, steamed (not French-cut)

Salt and pepper to taste

2 tablespoons beef bouillon granules, or 2 beef bouillon cubes

1 clove garlic, minced

Directions

Over medium heat, sauté onions in oil and butter. Add tomatoes, beef bouillon and garlic. Bring mixture to a boil. Cook for about 5 minutes or until

onions are soft. Add green beans. Cook 5 minutes longer or until heated through, or beans are cooked if using fresh or frozen. If necessary add a small amount of water to keep beans moist. Serves 8.

Veggie Bake

A hearty flavorful dish that is perfect for a winter day, served with meat, fish or chicken and Buttery Biscuit Sticks. Everything can bake in the oven at once. (Shown paired with Zucchini Sausage Bake recipe on page 18.)

Ingredients

1–2 lbs. green and red peppers

1 lb. potatoes and/or yams, peeled

1 large onion, peeled

3 large carrots, peeled

1 clove garlic, crushed

¼ cup olive oil

Salt and pepper to taste

2 tablespoons Italian herbs

Directions

Preheat oven to 425 degrees. Trim and clean peppers, cut into 1½-inch vertical slices. Cut potatoes into thick chunks. Cut onions into thick vertical slices. Cut peeled carrots into thick slices.

Place vegetables and garlic in large roasting pan, such as used to roast a turkey. Add oil and seasonings, toss to combine thoroughly. Bake, uncovered, turning occasionally, 30–45 minutes, or until potatoes and carrots are tender. Serves 6–8.

Serving suggestion: Italian Eggplant (p. 9), Rice Pudding (p. 61)

Oven-Baked Fries

When the baking potatoes have sprouted, dried out a little and developed spots, they are no longer suitable for baking. That's when this recipe comes in handy. Waste not want not!

Ingredients

3 large baking potatoes or sweet potatoes

2 tablespoons olive oil

1 teaspoon paprika

1 teaspoon salt

¼ teaspoon pepper

Directions

Preheat oven to 400 degrees. Spray cookie sheet with non-stick spray. Wash and peel baking potatoes. Cut into halves, then fourths, then eighths. Cut out any brown spots or discoloring. Lay out on cookie sheet. Sprinkle olive oil over all, then paprika, salt and pepper.

Place in 400-degree oven and bake for 30 minutes. Pull out and turn each piece. Return to oven and bake an additional fifteen minutes. Serves 4.

Serving Suggestion: Massachusetts Clam Chowder (p. 15), Golden Squash Bake (p. 31)

Herb-roasted Potatoes

Ingredients

⅓ cup Dijon mustard

2 tablespoons olive oil

1 clove garlic, chopped

½ teaspoon Italian herbs

6 medium potatoes (red are good but you can use any kind), cut into chunks

Directions

Mix all ingredients except potatoes in small bowl. Place potatoes in lightly greased 13 x 9″ pan and cover with seasoning mixture.

Bake at 425 degrees for 35–40 minutes or until potatoes are fork tender, stirring occasionally. Serves 4–6.

Serving suggestions: Cajun Pot Roast (p. 21), Roasted Garlic (p. 34)

Roasted Garlic

Ingredients

2 whole heads fresh garlic, unpeeled

¼ teaspoon salt

3 tablespoons olive oil

Directions

Preheat oven to 425 degrees. Cut ¼–½ inch off the pointed ends of the garlic heads, enough to expose the garlic cloves. Put the heads of garlic in a custard cup or ramekin. Pour the olive oil on the open ends of garlic and sprinkle with salt. Cover and cook in 425-degree oven for about 45 minutes, the same time it takes to bake a large potato.

Squeeze soft garlic over roast meat, baked potatoes or bread. Serves 4.

Serving suggestion: For a complete but easy dinner, cook the garlic and baking potatoes at the same time; serve with grated cheese and steamed broccoli for toppings.

Fried Green Tomatoes

Gather the large green and half-ripe tomatoes from the garden before the first frost. Many recipes exist for using them. Our two favorites are Fried Green Tomatoes and Green Tomato Pie, which is in the dessert section of this book.

Ingredients

8 medium tomatoes, green or half-ripe

1 cup flour

1½ teaspoon salt

1½ tablespoon sugar

½ teaspoon pepper

1 can evaporated milk

Oil for frying

Directions

Wash tomatoes but do not peel. Cut into ¾ inch slices. Place slices on paper towels to drain. Combine flour, salt, sugar and pepper. Dust tomatoes in flour mixture on both sides. Add evaporated milk to remaining flour mixture to make a thick batter. Dip floured tomatoes in batter. Fry in hot oil ½-inch deep in pan until golden brown on both sides. Serves 6.

Serving suggestion: Cajun Pot Roast (p. 21), Rice Pudding (p. 61)

Favorite Zucchini

Because everything is better with bacon and cheese.

Ingredients

2 strips uncooked bacon, cut in pieces

5 or 6 medium unpeeled zucchini, cut in chunks

1 small onion, chopped

1 large tomato, peeled and chopped

Pinch of sugar

Salt and pepper to taste

½ cup Monterey jack cheese, grated

Directions

Place bacon in saucepan, add all other ingredients except for cheese. Cover tightly and simmer for 15–20 minutes, or until zucchini is tender. Add cheese just before serving. Serves 4.

Relief Society Potatoes

These are also called funeral potatoes, because they are comfort food that can feed a crowd. They were a big hit with my teenage boys. This is the small recipe. I would triple it and use regular onions, which I always keep on hand, instead of green onions.

Ingredients

1 2 lb. bag of frozen hash brown potatoes, thawed

1 10¾ oz. can cream of mushroom soup

1 pint sour cream

1½ cup shredded cheddar cheese

⅓ cup chopped green onion

½ teaspoon salt

½ cup corn flakes, crushed

4 tablespoons melted butter

Directions

Preheat oven to 350 degrees. Lightly grease 9 x 13″ pan or casserole dish.

In large bowl mix together the thawed hash browns, cream of mushroom soup, sour cream, shredded cheese, onion and salt. Spread potato mixture into pan and smooth top.

In small bowl, thoroughly mix the crushed corn flakes and melted butter. Sprinkle this mixture over potato mixture. Bake uncovered for thirty or forty minutes, or until cheese is melted. Serves 6

Serving suggestion: Broccoli Salad (p. 29), Best Apple Crisp (p. 53)

Irish Potatoes

I seek out international recipes since they are indicative of cultures managing to survive through hard times. The addition of all the green onions in this recipe to what is essentially mashed potatoes, adds flavor, color and interest. The taste is similar to a baked potato with chives.

Ingredients

About 8 lbs potatoes, or ⅔ of a 10 lb. bag

1 tablespoon salt

3 bunches green onions

1 stick (½ cup butter)

Directions

Peel and chop the potatoes. Rinse, then put in large pan and cover with water and 1 tablespoon salt. Bring to boil then reduce to simmer and cook until tender. Pour off water into a separate bowl to save for later.

Chop the green onions. Put them in a microwave-safe bowl and add two cups of the reserved potato water. Microwave on high for 2 minutes.

Mash the potatoes by hand, adding the green onions and water; leave some lumps. Add more reserved potato water as needed. Add the butter and stir well until it melts throughout. Serves 8–10. Serve with additional butter and salt and pepper to taste.

Serving suggestion: Zucchini Sausage Bake (p. 10), Banana Nut Cake (p. 56)

Yeast Breads, Quick Breads, Grains

Pumpkin Raisin Muffins

Ingredients

2 cups flour

2 cups sugar

2 teaspoons baking soda

1 teaspoon nutmeg

2 teaspoons cinnamon

1 16 oz. can pumpkin

4 eggs

1 cup applesauce

⅓ cup water

1 teaspoon vanilla

1 cup chopped pecans or walnuts

1 cup raisins

Directions

Preheat oven to 350 degrees. Mix dry ingredients in large bowl. Set aside. In separate bowl beat pumpkin, eggs, applesauce, water and vanilla. Mix wet and dry ingredients. Stir in nuts and raisins.

Line muffin tin with cupcake papers. Fill each muffin cup ⅔ cup full. Bake for 25–30 minutes. Cool in pan for ten minutes. Makes 24 muffins.

Buttery Biscuit Sticks

Ingredients

½ stick (¼ cup) butter

⅓ cup shortening

1¾ cups flour

2½ teaspoons baking powder

½ teaspoon salt

½ cup milk

Directions

Heat oven to 450 degrees. Add butter to a 9-inch pie pan and heat in oven until melted, about two minutes. Remove pan and set aside.

Combine dry ingredients in mixing bowl. Cut in shortening with pastry cutter until mixture resembles fine crumbs. (If you don't have a pastry cutter, two or three table knives held together in one hand makes a suitable tool for cutting shortening into flour.)

Pour in milk and stir until dough leaves side of bowl and rounds into a ball. If too dry, add additional milk, a tablespoon at a time until you get desired results. You do not want the dough to be sticky.

Turn dough onto lightly floured surface. Knead lightly a few times; flatten into a circle about ¼ inch thick. Cut circle in half, then cut each half crosswise into one-inch wide strips. Dip strips in melted butter in pie plate, coating both sides, as you arrange the strips in pan. They will fit very tightly together.

Bake at 450 degrees until golden brown, about 10–12 minutes. Makes 12–16 sticks.

Poppy Seed Loaf

One of my sons learned to make this at a friend's house, and it became such a favorite of our family that I started buying poppy seeds in bulk. (*Note:* Don't eat this bread the day before a drug test)

Ingredients

1 cup milk

1½ teaspoons almond extract

½ cup oil

2 eggs

2½ cups flour

1 cup sugar

¼ cup poppy seeds

1 tablespoon baking powder

1 teaspoon salt

Glaze: ½ cup powdered sugar stirred into 2 tablespoons lemon juice

Directions

Preheat oven to 350 degrees. Grease bottom only of
a large bread loaf pan.

Mix liquid Ingredients milk, almond extract, oil,
egg. In separate bowl, combine dry Ingredients flour,
sugar, poppy seeds, baking powder and salt. Add
liquid ingredients to dry ingredients and stir just
enough to blend together. Pour batter into pan then
bake for 50–60 minutes, or until done (toothpick or
knife inserted in center comes out clean).

Remove from pan and while warm drizzle top with
glaze. Cool completely before slicing.

Honey Oat Bread

This is a sweet, moist yeast bread that makes wonderful toast. Instead of soaking oats in water, you
can use two to four cups of leftover cooked oatmeal.
I've done both methods with excellent results.

Ingredients

2 cups boiling water

2 cups rolled oats

2 packages (2 tablespoons) active dry yeast

⅔ cup warm water

½ cup honey

2 tablespoons oil

2 teaspoons salt

6 to 7 cups all-purpose flour (may use 2 or 3 cups
whole wheat flour in place of white)

Directions

In a large mixing bowl, combine boiling water and
oats; let stand until warm. In a small bowl, dissolve
yeast in warm water; add to oat mixture. Add honey,
oil, salt, and four cups flour; beat until smooth.
Add enough remaining flour to form a soft dough.
Turn out on a floured board or surface; knead until
smooth and elastic, about 6–8 minutes. Place in a

greased bowl, turning once to grease top. Cover and let rise in a warm place until doubled, about one hour. Punch the dough down. Shape into loaves and place in two greased loaf pans. Brush tops with melted butter and sprinkle with oats. Cover and let rise in warm place until doubled, about 30 minutes. Bakes at 350 degrees for 50–55 minutes or until golden brown.

Buttermilk Biscuits

A family favorite, delicious served with soup and stew, and a good way to use up milk that has gone sour. Yes, it's perfectly all right to use your sour milk in cooking, just be sure to add a teaspoon of baking soda with the dry ingredients when substituting sour milk for fresh in a bread recipe.

Ingredients

4 cups flour

4 teaspoons baking powder

1 teaspoon salt

1 teaspoon cream of tartar

1½ teaspoon baking soda

1 tablespoon sugar

1 cup shortening

1⅓ cup sour milk or buttermilk

Directions

Preheat oven to 450 degrees. In large bowl, add flour, baking powder, salt, cream of tartar, baking soda and sugar. Stir together well. Cut in shortening with pastry cutter until like coarse crumbs. Make a well in center of dough and add milk all at once. Stir quickly with fork until dough balls up and follows fork around bowl.

Turn onto lightly floured surface. Knead gently eight or ten times. Pat dough into a large circle one-half inch thick. Using biscuit cutter, make biscuits and place on ungreased cookie sheet. Bake at 450 degrees for 10–12 minutes. Makes about 32 medium biscuits.

Steamed White Rice

A rice cooker can be convenient but nothing beats the steamy sweetness of white rice cooked tenderly on top of the stove.

Ingredients

2 cups white rice

4 cups water

1 teaspoon salt

Directions

Thoroughly wash rice by placing in wire strainer and running cold water through it, lifting rice with fingers as it rinses, until the water runs nearly clear.

Add rice, water and salt to sauce pan. Heat to boiling, stirring once or twice; reduce heat. Cover pan and simmer eighteen minutes (set timer). Do not stir or lift lid during this time.

After timer goes off, remove pan from heat. Fluff rice lightly with fork. Cover and let steam for ten minutes. Serves 6.

Variation: For Brown Rice, follow these directions but double cooking time.

Maine Muffins

Home-made muffins are so much healthier and lower in calories than store-bought muffins. With fruit, nuts and even vegetables, these are chock full of added protein and nutrition. You'll want to make extra for quick breakfasts and snacks.

Ingredients

2 cups flour

1 cup sugar

2 teaspoons baking soda

1½ teaspoons cinnamon

½ teaspoon salt

3 eggs

½ cup vegetable oil

½ cup milk

1½ teaspoon vanilla

2 cups chopped, peeled apples

2 cups grated carrots

½ cup coconut

½ cup raisins

½ cup sliced almonds

Directions

Preheat oven to 375 degrees. In large bowl, combine flour, sugar, baking soda, cinnamon and salt. In another bowl, beat eggs, then add oil, milk and vanilla. Mix well. Stir into dry ingredients just until moistened. Fold in remaining ingredients.

Fill greased or lined muffin tins ¾ full. Bake at 375 degrees for 20–25 minutes, until done. They will be lightly browned and a knife or toothpick inserted in center will come out clean. Delicious with butter and honey.

Fruit and Nut Muffins

Double or triple this for extras. They're good with breakfast, with sack lunches and they also make a wonderful after-school snack.

Ingredients

1½ cups white flour

1 cup oats

½ cup brown sugar or honey

2 teaspoons baking powder

½ teaspoon salt

1 cup milk

1 egg

¼ cup oil

1 cup chopped dates, apples, or raisins, or a combination of the three

½ cup pecans or walnuts, chopped

Directions

Preheat oven to 375 degrees. Combine flour, oats, brown sugar, baking powder and salt. Stir together in mixing bowl. In a smaller bowl, whisk egg and oil together, add milk and pour into mixing bowl with dry ingredients. Add fruits and nuts and blend.

Drop into greased or lined muffin cups, filling ⅔ full. This is a heavy batter and will not raise a lot. Bake for 20 minutes. (Check after fifteen and take out if they are done. Check for doneness by sticking a toothpick in the top. It should come out dry.)

Take muffins out of pan and arrange on a serving plate or basket. Cover hot muffins with a tea towel to keep moist and warm until ready to serve. Serve with butter and jam or honey. Makes 12 muffins.

Serving suggestion: Red Beans and Rice (p. 14), Spinach Orange Salad (p. 28)

Nutty Muffins

A variation on Fruit and Nut Muffins, these also have a hearty, crunchy texture and make a wholesome snack. Keep a supply of muffins on hand for kids to grab, or to add to a meal. They're so easy to make, and better for you than cookies, brownies or cupcakes.

Ingredients

1½ cups white flour

1 cup oats

½ cup brown sugar or honey

2 teaspoons baking powder

½ teaspoon salt

1 cup milk

1 egg

½ cup chunky peanut butter

½ cup diced apples

½ cup raisins

½ cup sunflower seeds

Directions

Preheat oven to 375 degrees. Combine flour, oats, brown sugar, baking powder and salt in mixing bowl. Stir together. In smaller bowl, add egg and oil and whisk together. Add milk and stir. Pour wet ingredients into dry ingredients. Add fruit and nuts and blend together.

Drop into greased or lined muffin cups, filling them ⅔ cup full. Bake for 15–20 minutes. Makes 12 muffins.

Eggnog Muffins

Ingredients

½ cup butter or margarine, softened

¾ cup granulated sugar

2 eggs

1 teaspoon vanilla

2 teaspoons baking powder

1 teaspoon ground nutmeg

¼ teaspoon salt

2¼ cups flour

1 cup commercial eggnog

Topping: 1 tablespoon sugar mixed with ¼ teaspoon nutmeg

Directions

Preheat oven to 350 degrees. Line 24 muffin cups with cupcake paper liners, Christmas-themed if they're available.

In a medium-sized bowl, beat butter until creamy. Beat in sugar until pale and fluffy. Beat in eggs and extracts. Add the dry ingredients, using just half the flour; then half the eggnog. Add remaining flour and eggnog.

Scoop batter into cups, filling ¾ full, or enough to fill 24 cups. Sprinkle with sugar and nutmeg mixture. Bake at 350 degrees for 20–25 minutes or until golden brown. Cool slightly before serving.

Overnight Coffee Cake

Coffee cake was the fancy muffin of the Fifties. Housewives would make a bread-like cake with a cinnamon sugar/nut topping in their 9 x 13″ pans

and serve it with coffee at morning get-togethers in the neighborhood. In the Eighties, the coffee cake morphed into huge, high-fat muffins and "housewife" became an unpolitically-correct term for "stay-at-home-mom." I vote for the resurgence of the coffee cake, because it's less trouble to make than fancy muffins and a serving is lower in fat and calories. This recipe can be put together at night and baked the next morning for breakfast.

Ingredients

2 cups flour

1 teaspoon baking powder

1 teaspoon baking soda

1 teaspoon cinnamon

½ teaspoon salt

⅔ cup butter, softened

1 cup sugar

½ cup brown sugar, packed

2 eggs

1 cup sour milk (can be milk gone sour, or fresh milk with 1 tablespoon lemon juice added)

Topping

1 cup brown sugar

1 cup pecans or walnuts, chopped

1 tablespoon cinnamon

½ teaspoon nutmeg

Directions

Combine topping ingredients and set aside. In mixing bowl, cream together butter and sugars until light and fluffy. Add eggs, one at a time, beating well after each addition.

Stir or sift flour, baking powder, baking soda, cinnamon and salt in separate bowl. Add dry ingredients to mixing bowl alternately with sour milk, beating well after each addition. The batter will be extremely smooth and light.

Spread enough batter to cover bottom of a greased 9 x 13″ baking pan. Sprinkle half the topping mixture over batter. Cover with remaining batter and top with remaining topping mixture. Cover and refrigerate eight hours or overnight.

Bake at 350 degrees for 35–40 minutes or until done, with sides pulled away from pan and knife inserted in center coming out clean. Let set for ten minutes before cutting in squares. It is very crumbly and tender; lift out carefully with spatula onto individual plates. Serve warm.

Serving suggestion: Have it for breakfast with scrambled eggs, hot cocoa, and cut up fruit.

Dad's Cornbread

Ingredients

2 cups flour

¾ cup sugar

2½ tablespoons baking powder

2 teaspoons baking soda (only if you are using sour milk or buttermilk)

1½ teaspoons salt

2 cups yellow cornmeal

4 eggs

2 cups milk, sour milk or buttermilk (if using fresh milk, do not add baking soda)

½ cup oil

Directions

Preheat oven to 425 degrees. Grease a 9 x 13" baking pan. Stir flour with sugar, baking powder, baking soda (if using sour milk), and salt. Stir in cornmeal. In separate bowl, whisk together eggs, milk and oil. Pour into dry ingredients and blend until smooth; do not overbeat. Pour mixture into greased baking pan. Bake at 425 degrees for 20–25 minutes.

Serving suggestion: Serve with any of the bean dishes or soups

Mom's Cornbread

Sweeter, less coarse, cake-like cornbread

Ingredients

2 cups flour

1½ cups sugar

2½ teaspoon baking powder

1½ teaspoon salt

2 cups white cornmeal

4 eggs

2 cups fresh milk, 2% or whole

½ cup melted butter

Directions

Preheat oven to 425 degrees. Grease a 9 x 13" baking pan. Stir together the dry ingredients. In separate bowl, whisk together eggs, milk and melted butter. Pour wet ingredients into dry and blend just until smooth; do not overbeat. Pour mixture into greased baking pan. Bake at 425 degrees for 25–30 minutes.

Serving suggestion: The sweeter cornbread is especially good with a spicy dish, like Red Beans and Rice (p. 14)

Scottish Oat Scones

This scone recipe is quick to make, and the dough is baked not fried. Good for breakfast. (The dough is very tasty, too.)

Ingredients

¼ cup butter, melted

⅓ cup milk

1 egg

1½ cups flour

1½ cup quick rolled oats, uncooked

¼ cup sugar

1 tablespoon baking powder

1 teaspoon cream of tartar

½ teaspoon salt

½ cup raisins

⅓ cup butter; ⅓ cup honey

Directions

Preheat oven to 425 degrees. Combine flour, oats, sugar, baking powder, cream of tartar and salt together in a bowl. Set aside.

Beat egg in small bowl; stir in ¼ cup melted butter and ⅓ cup milk. Add to dry ingredients and stir just until blended. The dough should be dry but add another tablespoon of milk if needed. Stir in raisins.

Pat out dough on greased cookie sheet to form an eight-inch circle about ½ inch thick. Cut into 8–12 wedges. Bake at 425 degrees for 12–15 minutes or until light golden brown. Remove from oven and cut through the pre-cooked scoring; let set for 5–10 minutes, then remove to serving platter.

Melt ⅓ cup butter and stir into ⅓ cup honey; drizzle over the top of the scones. Serve with any leftover honey/butter mixture.

Serving suggestion: Have for breakfast with scrambled eggs and hot cocoa; or as bread with any meal.

Easy Pumpkin Bread

This recipe can be made fast and easy, all in one mixing bowl, has no added oil and is a favorite for snacking at our house. Delicious spread with peanut butter or cream cheese.

Ingredients

1 16 oz. can applesauce

4 cups sugar

8 eggs

1 29 oz. can pumpkin

1⅓ cups water

6⅔ cups flour

4 teaspoons baking soda

1 tablespoon salt

1 teaspoon baking powder

2 teaspoons ground cinnamon

2 teaspoons ground cloves

1½ teaspoons pumpkin pie spice

3 cups raisins

2 cups pecans or walnuts

Directions

Preheat oven to 350 degrees. Grease four large loaf pans. Add ingredients in order given in a large bowl, blending well after each addition. Pour mixture into four loaf pans. Bake at 350 degrees for one hour, ten minutes; or longer if needed. When done, knife stuck in center will come out clean. Cool completely before removing from pans. Makes 4 large loaves.

Ricotta Garlic Bread

This bread truly tastes too good to be this easy.

Ingredients

10 cloves garlic, finely minced

1 cup ricotta cheese (nonfat is fine)

⅓ cup olive oil

½ cup parsley, finely chopped

¼ teaspoon red pepper flakes

¼ teaspoon salt

1 long loaf Italian or French bread

Directions

Preheat oven to 350 degrees. Mix the minced garlic, ricotta, olive oil, parsley, salt and red pepper flakes together. Slice the bread lengthwise and place on a sheet of heavy duty foil. Spread both halves with ricotta mixture. Place the halves back together and wrap tightly in the foil. Bake 30 minutes at 350 degrees.

Remove from oven and carefully unwrap. Cut into one-inch thick sandwich chunks.

Granola Cereal

Yes, you *can* make your own cereal!

Ingredients

6 cups rolled oats

1 cup wheat germ

½ cup coconut

½ cup sesame seeds

½ cup chopped nuts

½ cup sunflower seeds

2 teaspoons cinnamon

½ cup vegetable oil

½ cup water

½ cup honey

½ cup molasses or brown sugar

1½ teaspoon vanilla

Directions

Preheat oven to 275 degrees. Combine oats, wheat germ, coconut, seeds, nuts and cinnamon in a large mixing bowl. Mix oil, water, honey, molasses or brown sugar on stove top and heat while stirring, until sugars are dissolved. Do not boil. Remove from heat, add vanilla, and pour over dry ingredients. Stir well.

Spread granola out in one or two large, shallow pans and bake at 275 degrees for 45 minutes, or until it reaches the desired state of brownness and dryness. Stir every 15 minutes (set timer) while baking. When done, add one cup raisins or chopped dates, if desired. Allow to cool and store in airtight container.

Large Order of Pancakes

Ingredients

4 cups flour

2 tablespoons baking powder

½ teaspoon baking soda (for Buttermilk Pancakes)

1 teaspoon salt

4 eggs

4 cups milk (for Buttermilk Pancakes use sour milk, buttermilk or milk with 1 teaspoon lemon juice added)

½ cup oil

Directions

Stir together the flour, sugar, baking powder, baking soda and salt. Separate egg whites and beat whites until fluffy. Combine egg yolks, milk and oil. Stir into dry ingredients just until blended. Fold in egg whites to final batter, leaving a few fluffs.

For pancakes, cook on hot, greased griddle or frying pan, turning when the sides dry out and center bubbles begin to pop. For waffles, cook in waffle-maker. Serves 6–8.

Home-made Maple Syrup

Ingredients

1 cup water

½ cup white sugar

2 cups brown sugar

2 tablespoons maple-flavored extract

Directions

Bring the water, white sugar, and brown sugar to a boil in a saucepan over medium-high heat. Reduce heat to medium-low, and stir in the maple extract. Simmer 3 minutes longer.

Dumplings

Dumplings are cooked on top of bubbling stew or soup. I always double or triple this. They will thicken any soup you add them to, especially when reheating the leftovers.

Ingredients

3 tablespoons shortening

1½ cups flour

2 teaspoons baking powder

¾ teaspoon salt

¾ cup milk

Directions

Stir together flour, baking powder and salt. Cut shortening into this mixture until it resembles fine crumbs. Stir in milk; dough should be thick. Drop dough by spoonsful onto boiling hot soup or stew. Simmer, uncovered, for ten minutes. Cover pot and cook on low about ten minutes longer. Makes 8–10 dumplings.

Parsley Dumplings: Add 3 tablespoons snipped fresh parsley or chives to dry ingredients.

Herb Dumplings: Add 1 tablespoon herbs (sage, celery seed or thyme) to the dry ingredients. Sage is especially good and the one I prefer.

Serving suggestion: Flu-Busting Chicken Soup (p. 17), Mom's Cornbread (p. 45)

Home-made Egg Noodles

A hearty addition to home-made chicken soup and one of the easiest pastas to make, these noodles can be served anywhere you would use noodles or pasta.

Ingredients

4 eggs

2 teaspoons oil

3 tablespoons water

2⅔ cups flour

1 teaspoon salt

Directions

Mix all ingredients together in order given. Let stand ten minutes. Roll out to $\frac{1}{16}$ inch thin on well-floured surface. Sprinkle flour on top of dough as needed; dough shouldn't be sticky. Using a pizza cutter, cut into one-half inch wide strips. Let dry on wire racks about two hours or longer. Cook in boiling, salted water as you would any pasta.

Or you can toss them into soup without drying first. Add noodles to soup ten minutes before soup is ready to be served. (Make sure soup has come to a boil before adding noodles.) Stir noodles while adding and for a couple of minutes afterward to prevent them sticking together.

Serving suggestion: Add to Flu-busting Chicken Soup (p. 17) along with Herb Dumplings (p. 48)

Refrigerator Rolls/ Scones/Doughnuts/ Cinnamon Rolls

Ingredients

3 tablespoons yeast

3 cups milk, scalded

1 cup butter, softened

6 eggs

1 cup warm water

1 tablespoon salt

1 cup sugar

10 or more cups flour

Directions

Dissolve yeast in warm water; set aside. Add salt to scalded milk; cool to lukewarm. Cream butter and sugar until fluffy in large bowl. Add eggs and beat until blended. Stir in yeast and milk. Gradually add 3 to 4 cups flour and beat until smooth. Stir in remaining flour. Dough should be soft but not sticky; add more flour one-half cup at a time until right consistency. It can be sticky but not runny-sticky; no kneading is necessary, although you may need to do a lot of stirring.

Let dough rise in covered bowl for one hour. Knead down well. Cover with tight lid and refrigerate overnight.

Roll out cold dough to ½ inch thickness. Cut into 2½-inch rounds. Brush melted butter on rounds; fold each one in half and lightly press edges together. Place on pan with sides, a baking pan or cookie sheet. (A cookie sheet with no sides will cause butter to drip and smoke in the oven while baking.) Brush tops with melted butter. Let rise two hours or until double.

Bake at 350 degrees for twenty minutes. Makes 4 to 5 dozen.

For Fried Scones or Doughnuts: Before refrigerating dough, shape for scones by flattening or for doughnuts by punching a hole in the middle. Fry in medium hot oil. Set on paper towels to drain and sprinkle tops with powdered sugar.

For Cinnamon Rolls: Take a portion of the roll dough (after refrigerating) and roll out to a ¼-inch thick rectangle. Spread liberally with melted butter, then cover with a layer of brown sugar. Sprinkle cinnamon over all. From the long side, roll the dough up carefully into a long snake-shape. With sharp knife or pizza cutter, slice into two-inch sections. Set the sections in a buttered pan, cut side down. Take any brown sugar/cinnamon mixture that fell out during rolling and cutting and sprinkle over the top. There are no measurements given for the butter, brown sugar and cinnamon because it depends on how much of the dough used for cinnamon rolls, but more is better than less. Let rise until double; bake for 20 minutes at 350 degrees. While still warm in the pan, frost with any butter cream icing.

Desserts

Best Apple Crisp

Ingredients

6–8 medium apples, peeled and sliced thin

1½ cups rolled oats

1½ cups packed brown sugar

1 cup flour

2 teaspoons cinnamon

1 cup butter, softened slightly

Directions

Slice apples and place in 9 x 13″ pan. Mix flour and cinnamon in bowl. Cut in butter with pastry cutter until crumbly. Stir in brown sugar and oats until thoroughly mixed. Spread topping over apples.

Bake in preheated 350 degree oven for one hour, or until apples are tender and topping is brown and crisp. Serve warm with vanilla ice cream. Serves 6–8.

Cinnamon Apples

When the apples lose their freshness and nobody's eating them anymore, it's time to make Cinnamon Apples. And if you have young children who take just a few bites of an apple and are done, take what's left and make Cinnamon Apples. Why throw away perfectly good food when with a little effort you can make something yummy from it?

Ingredients

2 apples

¼ cup water

2 tablespoons sugar

1 teaspoon cinnamon

Directions

Peel apples and cut into thick slices. Drop into sauce pan; add water, sugar and cinnamon. Bring to boil, then reduce heat. Simmer on low until apples are tender. Serve with cream, or ice cream. Serves 2.

Hot Fudge Sauce or Hot Cocoa

Ingredients

⅓ cup regular dry cocoa

⅓ cup sugar

Dash salt

½ cup water

3½ cup milk, preferably 2% or whole

1 teaspoon vanilla

Directions

In saucepan, mix cocoa, sugar and salt; add water and blend mixture with a whisk on medium high. Bring to boiling, stirring constantly. Boil one minute; remove from heat. You now have hot fudge sauce to put on ice cream and you can stop right now. But if you want hot cocoa, return pan to heat and add the milk all at once. Stir and heat to boiling point *but do not boil.*

Remove pan from heat; add vanilla. Beat with whisk just before serving. Makes four cups.

Serving suggestion: Marshmallows, candy canes, chocolate mint cookies for dipping

Chocolate Oat Bars

I like having a few basic bar cookie recipes to use for after-school snacking, or quick desserts to jazz up a meal. I like this one because it has oatmeal for health and fiber, and chocolate and pecans for glamour.

Ingredients

1 cup flour

½ teaspoon cinnamon

1 cup (2 sticks) butter (*not* margarine), softened

½ cup sugar

½ cup brown sugar

1½ teaspoon vanilla

1 egg

1¼ cup quick oats, uncooked

2 cups real milk chocolate (*not* semi-sweet) chips, divided

¾ cups chopped pecans

Directions

Preheat oven to 350 degrees. Lightly grease 9 x 13″ pan.

Blend softened butter, sugars and vanilla in mixing bowl until creamy. Beat in egg. Gradually mix in flour and cinnamon; stir in oats and blend well. Add ¾ cup of the milk chocolate chips. Spread into prepared baking pan.

Bake at 350 degrees for 20–30 minutes, or until center is set. Immediately sprinkle with remaining 1¼ cup chocolate chips. (Be sure to use real, high quality milk chocolate chips. The cheap artificial kind will not melt no matter what you do.) Turn off oven and place pan on oven rack for ten minutes. Remove from oven and spread chocolate smooth; sprinkle with chopped nuts. Cool slightly before cutting.

Raisin Bars

A cookie recipe made all in a pot then poured into the baking pan. It is low-fat, sweet and spicy, a nice light snack.

Ingredients

1 cup raisins

1 cup water

¼ teaspoon salt

1 teaspoon baking soda

½ cup applesauce

1 cup sugar

1 teaspoon nutmeg

1 teaspoon allspice

1 teaspoon cinnamon

2 cups flour

2 eggs, beaten

½ cup chopped nuts

Powdered sugar

Directions

Preheat oven to 375 degrees. Grease a 9 x 13″ baking pan.

Combine raisins and water. Bring to boil. Remove from heat and add oil. Cool to lukewarm and stir in sugar and beaten egg. Combine dry ingredients and then add them to raisin mixture, beating well. Stir in nuts.

Pour into prepared pan and bake at 375 degrees for twenty minutes or until done. Dust with powdered sugar. When cool, cut into 24 large bars.

Coconut Lime Squares

A fancy bar cookie with a buttery crust, this is suitable for company dinner. For Lemon Squares, substitute lemon for lime.

Ingredients for Crust

1¾ cup flour

1½ stick (12 tablespoons or ¾ cup) cold butter, cut into bits

⅔ cup sweetened, flaked coconut

½ cup powdered sugar

¼ teaspoon salt

Ingredients for Custard

8 large eggs

2 cups sugar

⅔ cup flour

1¼ cup fresh lime juice, from about 10 limes

2 tablespoons freshly grated lime zest

⅔ cup sweetened, flaked coconut

Directions

Preheat oven to 325 degrees. Butter and flour a 9 x 13″ baking pan, knocking out excess flour.

For Crust: In a bowl, blend together the crust ingredients with pastry cutter or fingertips until mixture resembles coarse meal. Pat into prepared pan and bake in middle of oven 25–30 minutes, or until golden brown. Remove and reduce oven temperature to 300 degrees.

For Custard: In mixer bowl, beat eggs and sugar until combined well. Stir in flour, lime juice and zest; beat well until smooth. Pour custard mixture over crust and bake in middle of 300 degrees oven for 20 minutes. Top custard with coconut and bake 5–10 minutes more, or until just set. Cool pan on a rack and then chill for at least one hour in refrigerator.

Cut into squares. Makes 32 two-inch squares.

Pineapple Upside Down Cake

This can also be used substituting canned apricots for the pineapple, then use the apricot juice instead of pineapple juice. It's an easy, inexpensive cake that will make a simple family meal seem special.

Ingredients

4 eggs

1 cup granulated sugar

⅔ cup pineapple juice

2 teaspoons vanilla

2 cups flour

1 teaspoon baking powder

2 teaspoons cinnamon, divided

½ teaspoon salt

½ cup (1 stick) butter

1 cup brown sugar

Directions

Preheat oven to 350 degrees. Add butter to 9 x 13″ baking dish and melt in heated oven. Sprinkle the melted butter with one cup brown sugar.

Beat eggs until thick. Gradually beat in granulated sugar. Add pineapple juice and vanilla. Add flour, baking powder, salt and ½ teaspoon cinnamon and beat for 2 minutes.

Arrange pineapple halves in two rows in baking dish. (If using apricot halves, place them cut side up.) Pour cake batter over fruit. Bake at 350 degrees for 35–40 minutes or until done.

Remove from oven and immediately turn upside down on serving platter. Do not remove pan for a few minutes to allow steam to soften and loosen cake. Best served warm with vanilla ice cream, or cold with whipped cream.

Banana Nut Cake

A very large cake that's great for company. A basic, easy to mix recipe, it's rich and delicious. Freezes well.

Ingredients

5 cups flour

2⅔ cups granulated sugar

6 medium, overly-ripe bananas (about 2½ cups mashed)

1⅓ cups sour cream

6 eggs

2½ teaspoons baking powder

2½ teaspoons baking soda

2 teaspoons salt

1½ cups chopped walnuts or pecans

Directions

Preheat oven to 350 degrees. Grease two 9 x 13″ baking pans, or one large roasting pan, 12 x 16″.

Add ingredients in order given (except for nuts) and beat together in large mixer bowl on low speed for one minute. Beat on high for three minutes. Stir in nuts. Pour batter into prepared pan.

Bake at 350 degrees for 45 minutes to one hour, or until pick in center comes out clean. Frost with Vanilla Butter Frosting when cake is cool.

Vanilla Butter Frosting

Ingredients

6 cups powdered sugar

⅔ cup butter, softened

1 tablespoon vanilla

¼ cup milk

Blend butter into powdered sugar. Stir in vanilla and milk; beat well until frosting is smooth and of spreading consistency. Add more milk by table-spoonful as needed.

Pistachio Pudding Cake

I have a lot of cake recipes because with ten children, we had a lot of birthdays. Although prepared cake mixes are easy and taste fine, a cake from scratch really isn't difficult to put together and makes the event seem more special. Warning: This is the richest cake I've ever had in my entire life. I've always said it should come with a warning label, so here it is. With the butter and cream content, and the inch-thick frosting, it's incredibly rich and should be cut into small pieces, no seconds allowed, and skip the ice cream.

Ingredients

2¼ cups flour

1⅔ cup sugar

2 cups milk

4 teaspoons baking powder

1 teaspoon salt

2 small packages instant pistachio pudding mix

1½ sticks butter, melted

5 eggs

2 teaspoons vanilla

Directions

Preheat oven for 350 degrees. Grease a 9 x 13″ pan, and also prepare a cupcake pan with liners. (This is too much batter for the 9 x 13″ pan) so I make 8–10 cupcakes as well.)

Add ingredients in order listed in mixing bowl and mix well at medium speed until thoroughly blended, for 2–4 minutes. Stop part way through to scrape the sides of bowl. Pour batter into prepared pans. Bake at 350 degrees for 35–45 minutes. Frost when cool. I have never yet been able to keep the middle from falling on this cake, but no matter. This frosting recipe covers it so thickly that you don't notice a sunken middle when you're done spreading it.

Pistachio Frosting

Ingredients

1 small package instant pistachio pudding

2 cups heavy whipping cream

3 cups powdered sugar

¼ cup butter, softened

Stir pudding into one cup of the heavy cream and let set for a few minutes. Then add remaining ingredients along with rest of cream and beat until fluffy. Spread onto cooled cake.

Variation

Coconut Cream Cake—Make as directed throughout, substituting instant coconut pudding mix for the pistachio, including the frosting recipe. After frosting, sprinkle top of cake liberally with sweetened, flaked coconut.

Famous Texas Cake

A family favorite, our kids grew up loving this cake. One time one of our sons said, "I bet I could eat a whole Texas cake." Of course I had to take him up on the challenge and bake one for him. He ate about three large pieces before deciding to share with his brothers and sisters, who were hovering around waiting for their chance.

Ingredients

2¼ cups flour

2 cups granulated sugar

1 teaspoon cinnamon

1 teaspoon baking soda

2 sticks (1 cup) butter

¼ cup cocoa

1 cup water

½ cup buttermilk or sour milk (milk with a teaspoon lemon juice added)

2 eggs, whisked with a fork

2 teaspoons vanilla

Directions

Preheat oven to 400 degrees. In large bowl, stir together flour, sugar, cinnamon and baking soda and set aside. In sauce pan, melt together butter, cocoa and water; bring to a boil. Pour the hot mixture over dry ingredients and stir slightly just to blend. Add the buttermilk, eggs and vanilla. Stir until mixed thoroughly.

Pour cake batter into greased cookie sheet with sides (16 x 12 x 1"). It will be runny. Bake at 400 degrees about 20 minutes, until sides pull away from the edges and toothpick inserted in center comes out clean. Frost while cake is still hot. Cut and serve when icing cools.

Texas Cake Frosting

Ingredients

1 stick butter, softened

2 tablespoons cocoa

⅓ cup milk

1 teaspoon vanilla

4½ cups powdered sugar

Combine butter, cocoa and milk in saucepan and bring to a boil, stirring constantly. Boil for one minute only; remove from heat. Measure powdered sugar into bowl. Pour chocolate mixture over powdered sugar and stir to blend slightly. Add vanilla and mix well until smooth and lump-free. Icing will be thin; no need to add more powdered sugar. Spread on warm Texas cake. Cool to allow icing to set before serving.

Lemonade Cake

This is a quick and easy recipe, definitely ones the kids can handle. It's light and tart and makes a wonderful dessert to go with a meat and potatoes-type meal. It freezes well since there's no icing, and it is even good served frozen.

Ingredients

1 lemon cake mix

1 (12 oz.) can frozen lemonade, thawed

⅔ cup powdered sugar

Directions

Prepare cake mix as directed on package, except substitute ⅓ cup lemonade mix for ⅓ cup water. Pour into a greased 9 x 13″ pan. Bake as directed on cake mix. Cool for fifteen minutes.

Mix remaining lemonade concentrate with powdered sugar. Prick cake all over with a fork and pour lemonade/sugar mixture over top. Allow to completely cool before cutting.

Orange Spice Cake

This cake can be mixed by hand. It's not overly sweet or rich, and has an interesting blend of flavors.

Ingredients

2½ cup flour

2 teaspoons baking powder

1 teaspoon baking soda

1 teaspoon salt

2 teaspoons cinnamon

½ teaspoon cloves

3 eggs

½ cup oil

1⅓ cup granulated sugar

½ cup orange juice

1 teaspoon almond extract

1½ cup grated carrots

Directions

Preheat oven to 350 degrees. Grease 9 x 13″ baking pan. In large bowl mix flour, baking powder, baking soda, salt, cinnamon and cloves. Set aside. With whisk beat eggs. Stir in oil, sugar, orange juice, almond extract and grated carrots. Mix well. Add to flour mixture, stirring just to moisten. Pour into prepared pan and bake at 350 degrees for

35–40 minutes. Frost with Orange Icing when cake is cool.

Orange Icing

Ingredients

2 tablespoons softened butter

3 cups powdered sugar

¼ cup orange juice

2 teaspoons lemon juice

Zest of one orange

In small bowl, combine all ingredients and beat together until creamy. Frost cooled cake.

Easy Chocolate Cake

A family favorite, this is a large cake. Like the other cakes included, it's easy to mix; add ingredients and mix in order given, making it fast and simple.

Ingredients

1½ cups water

1 cup shortening

6 large eggs

3 tablespoons vanilla

2½ cups flour

2½ cups granulated sugar

1½ cups unsweetened cocoa powder

3 teaspoons baking powder

½ teaspoon baking soda

½ teaspoon salt

Directions

Preheat oven to 350 degrees. Grease a large baking pan (12 x 16″) or 2 baking pans (9 x 13″).

Combine ingredients in order given and mix thoroughly with electric mixer on low, then blend on high speed another three minutes. Batter should be light and fluffy. Spread in prepared pan and bake for 35–40 minutes, or until pick inserted in center comes out clean. Frost when cool, or still slightly warm for easy spreading.

Chocolate Butter Frosting

Ingredients

4 cups powdered sugar

½ cup unsweetened cocoa powder

½ cup butter, softened

1 teaspoon vanilla

½ cup canned, evaporated milk

Blend butter into powdered sugar and cocoa. Add vanilla and milk. Beat well until light and fluffy. Add additional milk by tablespoonful if needed for consistency. Spread frosting evenly on cooled cake. Double the frosting recipe if you like your cakes thickly frosted.

Deliciously Decadent Brownies

Ingredients

1½ cup butter, softened

3 cups sugar

1 tablespoon vanilla

5 large eggs

2 cups flour

1 cup unsweetened cocoa powder

½ teaspoon salt

1½ cup chopped nuts, if desired

Directions

Preheat oven to 350 degrees. Cream butter and sugar with electric mixer. Add vanilla and blend in eggs until smooth. Set aside. Sift or stir together flour, cocoa and salt. Add dry ingredients to creamed mixture. Stir to blend and then mix on medium speed until batter is light and fluffy.

Spread batter into Texas cake pan (a cookie sheet with sides). Batter will be thick and fudgey. It is rich and delicious, people will be lining up to lick the beaters and the mixing bowl.

Bake at 350 degrees for 20 minutes. When cool, spread with Chocolate Butter Frosting and sprinkle the chopped nuts on top. The Chocolate Butter Frosting recipe makes just the right amount to thickly cover the brownies.

Maple Bars

This is a complicated, time-consuming recipe compared to the other ones in this book, and you'll need an assistant in the kitchen. But if you love a good, fresh maple bar and want to try making them yourself it is well worth the trouble. We have a tradition of gathering on Thanksgiving Eve for soup and maple bars.

Ingredients

1½ cups milk

½ cup shortening

¼ cup granulated sugar

2 teaspoons salt

2 tablespoons yeast

¼ cup warm water

4¾ cups flour

3 eggs, beaten well

1 cup oil or amount needed to fry the dough

Directions

Bring milk to boiling point but do not boil. Pour over shortening, sugar and salt in a large bowl. Cool to lukewarm. Dissolve yeast in warm water and add to lukewarm mixture along with flour and eggs; mix well.

Turn dough out into greased bowl, turning once to grease top. Cover and let rise in warm place until doubled. Punch down. Place on well-floured board and roll out to one-half inch thickness. Cut into 2"x 4" pieces. A pizza cutter works well for this. Lay the cut rectangles out on flat pans and cover. Let rise until double.

Heat oil in deep skillet or fryer to 375 degrees. Fry dough rectangles a few at a time until golden on all sides. Remove to paper towels to drain, and then move back to flat pans to frost. Frost while they are still warm.

Maple Frosting

Ingredients

1½ cup powdered sugar

3 tablespoons butter, softened

¼ cup milk

1 tablespoon maple extract

Measure powdered sugar, butter, and maple extract into bowl. Add milk, one tablespoon at a time, and mix well until frosting is smooth and spreadable. Spread on warm maple bars.

Rice Pudding

Made in the slow cooker for convenience this is a good way to use leftover white rice. Packed full of milk and eggs, it makes a suitable breakfast, cold or hot. I always double it.

Ingredients

2½ cups cooked white rice

1 can evaporated milk

⅔ cup brown or white sugar

3 tablespoons butter

2 teaspoons vanilla

½ teaspoon nutmeg

3 eggs, beaten well

½ cup raisins, optional

Directions

Thoroughly combine rice with all remaining ingredients except raisins. Pour into lightly greased slow cooker. Cover and cook on high 2 hours or low 4–6 hours. Stir after the first hour and as needed. Add raisins if desired the last couple hours of cooking.

The rice pudding will be thick and eggy. Mix it together with leftover rice at night, set on low and have it in the morning for breakfast, like a hot cereal.

Butterscotch Dumplings

For when you want a nice dessert but don't have any fancy ingredients for nice desserts, this one is utterly decadent, especially with cream. Serve in dessert dishes with cream pitcher on the side. (Pictured on page 59.)

Ingredients for Sauce

¼ cup butter

2 cup brown sugar

1 cup granulated sugar

3 cups water

¼ teaspoon salt

Ingredients for Dumplings

3 cup flour

1 tablespoon baking powder

1 cup granulated sugar

½ teaspoon salt

¼ cup butter, melted

1 cup milk

1 teaspoon vanilla

Directions

For Sauce: Combine butter, sugars, water and salt in saucepan. Bring to a boil, simmer for five minutes. While sauce is simmering, make dumplings.

For Dumplings: Combine dumpling ingredients and mix well. Form into about 25 small balls and drop into simmering sauce. Cover and cook for 20 minutes without lifting lid. Serve warm with cream. Serves 8.

Family Flan

I used to order flan in Mexican restaurants and treasure every delicious bite, thinking it was too difficult to make at home. Oh boy was I wrong. This method is easy and serves not just one but the whole family. And it tastes just as good as flan in the expensive restaurants.

Ingredients

8 eggs

⅔ cup granulated sugar

¼ teaspoon salt

3½ cups evaporated milk (about 3 12-oz. cans)

2 teaspoons vanilla

1 cup light brown sugar

Directions

Preheat oven to 350 degrees. Beat eggs until yolks and whites are well-blended. Add granulated sugar and salt. Beat in evaporated milk and vanilla.

Sprinkle brown sugar in bottom of bread loaf pan; gently pour custard over brown sugar. Place loaf pan in shallow baking pan containing hot water. Bake for one hour in 350 degrees oven until knife inserted in center comes out clean.

Refrigerate overnight. Run knife around edge of pan and turn out onto small, oven-proof platter. If you don't have the right platter, you can fit flan into a ten-inch pie plate; may need to cut off ends so it fits.

Bring to room temperature. Before serving place under broiler and brown for approximately 5–10 minutes. Watch carefully and do not burn. Slice carefully and gently ease slices onto dessert plates. Serves 10.

Bread Pudding with Vanilla Sauce

I save stale bread like heels, half slices, random buns and rolls in a plastic bag in the freezer. When there's enough, I make bread pudding. Made with bread, milk and eggs, it's suitable for breakfast; with the Vanilla Sauce it's a low-fat, low-sugar dessert.

Ingredients

2¼ cups milk

2 slightly beaten eggs

2 cups bread cubes

½ cup brown sugar

1 teaspoon cinnamon

1 teaspoon vanilla

½ teaspoon salt

½ cup raisins (if desired)

Directions

Preheat oven to 350 degrees. Combine milk and eggs. Pour over the bread cubes. Add the brown sugar, cinnamon, vanilla, salt and raisins. Toss to blend. Spread mixture in a square glass baking dish (8 x 8 x 2″). Set dish in a shallow pan on oven rack. Pour water into shallow pan up to one inch deep. Bake for 50–60 minutes or until knife inserted in center comes out clean. Serves 6. Serve with Vanilla Sauce and sprinkle top with cinnamon.

Vanilla Sauce

Ingredients

½ cup light brown sugar

1 tablespoon flour

½ teaspoon cinnamon

1 egg

2 tablespoons butter

1¼ cups 2% or whole milk

Pinch salt

1 tablespoon vanilla

Combine sauce ingredients (except vanilla) in heavy saucepan and cook over medium heat, stirring rapidly with a whisk until thoroughly blended. Continue stirring with a spoon until sauce bubbles and thickens. Stir in vanilla extract. Serve over warm bread pudding; sprinkle with cinnamon before serving.

Directions

Bake pie crust according to directions.

Preheat oven at 400 degrees. Combine ingredients in saucepan in order given. Cook on medium heat until thick, stirring constantly. Pour into baked pie shell. Cover with meringue and brown slightly at 400 degrees, for about five minutes. Watch closely, do not burn.

Meringue

Beat the three egg whites until light and fluffy. Add ¼ cup granulated sugar and beat well. Top pie with meringue and bake as instructed.

Amber Pie

Something different, sweet and spicy, Amber Pie is best in a home-made pie crust, but works well in a prepared one if that's your best option. Because sometimes life calls for pie.

Ingredients

Pastry for 9″ pie

1 cup raisins

2 tablespoons butter

½ teaspoon nutmeg

½ teaspoon cloves

½ teaspoon cinnamon

¼ teaspoon salt

2 tablespoons flour

3 tablespoons apple cider vinegar

1 cup buttermilk

1 cup granulated sugar

3 eggs, separated, saving out the whites

Green Tomato Pie

My pioneer ancestors would make pies from just about anything that was plentiful and in season. Fruit, of course, is a natural to go in dough and bake in the oven. Also meat, vegetables, milk and butter for pudding pies, and even green tomatoes.

Ingredients

Pastry for one 9″ pie, with either lattice crust or full top crust

6 medium green tomatoes

¾ cup golden raisins

1–2 teaspoons lemon zest

2 tablespoons lemon juice

1 tablespoon apple cider vinegar

1½ cup granulated sugar

3 tablespoons cornstarch

¼ teaspoon salt, scant

¼ teaspoon cinnamon

¼ teaspoon ginger

2 tablespoons butter

Directions

Line the pie plate with pastry and chill. Preheat oven to 425 degrees.

Wash the tomatoes and cut them into ⅛-inch slices, cutting the slices again into half-moons. Discard the stem ends. Put the tomato slices in a large mixing bowl and add the raisins, lemon zest and juice, and vinegar. Stir and set aside.

Combine the sugar, cornstarch, salt and spices in a small bowl. Sprinkle 2 tablespoons of this mixture over the chilled pie crust, and mix the rest with the sliced tomatoes. Turn the filling into the pie crust and dot with butter. It will be runny.

Cut the remaining pastry into ½-inch strips to make a criss cross design over the filling. Place five strips evenly over the pie filling, and place five more strips over them on the diagonal. Flute the edges of the pastry. Place the pie on a cookie sheet to catch the drips; bake pie for 15 minutes at 425 degrees. Reduce heat to 325 degrees and bake for another 50 minutes or until the filling is bubbling and the crust is golden brown. Let the pie cool completely before cutting.

Serving suggestion: It's pie. It goes with anything and everything.

Mincemeat Pie

This is a traditional harvest pie, using the abundance of the season to celebrate Thanksgiving or Christmas. I include it here for the record, because mincemeat didn't always come in a jar, and mincemeat pie really did used to have real beef in it. I made it a few times for a holiday meal, served along with pumpkin and apple pies, since mincemeat is an acquired taste and kids don't generally like it. But it's educational for them to understand how people used to put all kinds of things in pies, and worth having at least once.

Ingredients

Pastry for top and bottom of 9″ pie

3 cups tart apples, peeled and finely chopped

1 lb. ground beef

1 cup water

1 teaspoon salt

1 cup raisins

¼ cup light corn syrup

1 cup granulated sugar

¼ cup apple cider vinegar

⅛ teaspoon nutmeg

½ teaspoon cloves

½ teaspoon allspice

1 teaspoon cinnamon

Directions

Preheat oven to 375 degrees.

Cook ground beef in water and salt until browned. Drain well and measure out one cup. Return to pan. Prepare apples and add to pan of drained meat, along with all the remaining ingredients. Simmer 45 minutes or until thickened, stirring frequently. Remove from heat and cool. Put in prepared pie plate, top with crust and bake at 375 degrees until nicely browned, about thirty minutes. Cool slightly before cutting.

Serving suggestion: Thanksgiving Dinner! Best served warm with vanilla ice cream.

Index

About the Author

Born and raised in central Illinois, the daughter of a small town boy/Methodist minister from Indiana and a farm girl/school teacher from Nebraska, Karen Jones Gowen has down-to-earth Midwestern roots. Karen and her husband Bruce have lived in Utah, Illinois, California and Washington, currently residing near Salt Lake City. They are the parents of ten children. Not surprisingly, family relationships are a recurring theme in Gowen's writing. Visit Karen at her website karenjonesgowen.com for more recipes, essays on family life, and information about her books.

Acknowledgements

I had so much fun putting together this cookbook. It was fun to roll back the years and cook like it was 1986 when there were seven hungry kids in the house. It was fun to invite people for dinner to help my husband and I sample the goods. It was fun to work with Erin Gowen, my daughter-in-law, who was the photographer for most of the recipes.

I owe Erin a huge debt of gratitude, because she and her camera made my creations look way better than I ever remember them back when I was rushing around cooking a meal for a hungry family. And thanks to Natalie Gowen, another daughter-in-law talented with the camera, for her amazing shot of the two casseroles.

Thank you to Don Gee for the cover design. I knew it would be awesome in his capable hands. I appreciate my husband Bruce for his continued support. Again, without his support there's no way I could have completed another book.

CPSIA information can be obtained
at www.ICGtesting.com
Printed in the USA
BVHW022204101222
653949BV00010B/471